MW01075976

Baha'i

STUDIES IN CONTEMPORARY RELIGIONS

Volumes in Print:

Additional volumes to follow.

Baha'i

Margit Warburg

STUDIES IN CONTEMPORARY RELIGIONS

Massimo Introvigne, Series Editor

Signature Books
in cooperation with CESNUR
(Center for Studies on New Religions)

© 2001 Elle Di Ci, Leumann (Torino), Italy.

Originally published in Italian as *I baha'i*, the current edition was updated by the author and adapted to a more general reading audience.

Published by arrangement with the copyright holder.

Published in the United States of America by Signature Books. Signature Books is a registered trademark of Signature Books Publishing, LLC.

www.signaturebooks.com

Cover design by Ron Stucki

LIBRARY OF CONGRESS CATALOGING-IN-PUBLICATION DATA
Warburg, Margit.
   [Baha'i. English]
   Baha'i / by Margit Warburg
     p. cm. -- (Studies in contemporary religions ; 5)
   "In cooperation with CENSUR (Center for Studies
     on New Religions.")
   Includes bibliographical references (p.).
   ISBN 1-56085-169-4 (pbk.)
   1. Baha'i Faith. I. Title. II. Series.

 BP365.W3713 2003
 299.9'3--dc21

                              2003045575

Contents

1.

The Baha'is

The building is in a quiet, central part of the city. A polished brass plaque next to the heavy entrance door reads "Bahá'í Centro." We enter, climb the stairs, and find a large, upper-middle-class apartment. It is sparsely but neatly furnished with slightly old-fashioned furniture. Above a small table with a lace centerpiece hangs a portrait of a white-bearded Middle Eastern man wearing a white turban and a long cloak. On other walls are pictures of characteristically nine-sided temples.

We are warmly received by four men and women, two who are native to the country, one Iranian, and another of distinctly Nordic appearance. The place is Palermo, Sicily, but it could be anywhere: a small shop in a busy street in Seoul, a modern concrete apartment in Reykjavik, a plastered turn-of-the-century villa in a well-to-do neighborhood in northern Copenhagen, a whitewashed, well-kept house on a dusty, littered road close to the American embassy in Banjul, Gambia, or an impressive complex of buildings below the tall, white, nine-sided temple on the shores of Lake Michigan near Chicago. They all share with the Palermo apartment the status of being the headquarters of a local Baha'i community, a so-called *Haziratu'l-Quds*, Arabic for "the sacred fold."[1]

Baha'is strive to represent every nationality and ethnic and linguistic group. They are united in a religion which is global in doctrine and scope. The religion was founded in Iran, but its headquarters and holiest sites are in Israel. Its historical origin is represented by the Shrine of the Bab half-way up the slope of Mount Carmel, overlooking Haifa. The pale, sandy, intricately carved structure with its stunning golden dome houses the remains of the Iranian religious leader Muhammad Ali Shirazi, also known as "the Bab" (1819-1850). The Bab was executed in Iran in 1850 for claiming to be the prophet whose message would supercede Islam and guide humankind into a new era. He gave rise to a revolutionary religious movement known as Babism that clashed with the Iranian government and collapsed after heavy fighting with government troops. The movement was reinvigorated in the 1860s under the leadership of the prophet Husain Ali Nuri (1817-1892), known as "Baha'u'llah," who developed Babism into Baha'i.

Behind the Shrine of the Bab, further up the mountain, stretches a large garden surrounded by a tall fence. Steeply banked, the garden attracts attention by its cypress groves, lush green lawns (a rare sight in the dry climate of Israel!), and winding gravel paths. A driveway leads to another imposing edifice, a three-storied colonnaded building made of white marble. This is the administrative headquarters of the religion, the "Seat of the Universal House of Justice." Here religious zeal blends with the daily tasks of running a modern religious organization reflected by exquisite interior decorations—dark wooden panels, Persian carpets, and mirror-polished flagstones in the central hall—and the business-like atmosphere of computers, telephones, desk files, and clipboards.

Baha'i is one of the oldest of the "new religions of the west." It appeared in the United States in the 1890s and reached Europe around 1900. In contrast to many other new non-Christian groups that have grown mainly as a result of immigration from outside the west, Baha'is in Europe and North America are predominantly native-born. The religion tends to be less well known than other new religions, however. In Europe and North America, Baha'is have escaped tabloid headlines: they are not reputed for zealous or colorful proselytizing efforts, nor have they been accused of brainwashing or dubious economic transactions. Indeed, it is hard to find any public animosity against them in the west.

However, the religion is highly controversial in most Muslim countries, in particular in Iran. After all, it has only been 150 years since the Babis in Iran threatened the government and were crushed in a brutal reprisal. Occasionally, prejudice still ignites into persecution in Iran. After Ayatollah Khomeini came to power in 1979, he systematically imprisoned and executed leading Baha'is, resulting in several condemnations from the United Nations. The reasons for arresting Baha'is were varied, but it was chiefly because of their belief that Baha'u'llah was God's manifestation on earth that they were arrested and executed. This belief is seen as heresy.

This book tells the complex and interesting story of the Baha'is. Their growth since the 1960s has been remarkable, culminating in a claimed membership of about five million worldwide. The Bahai'is believe that their religion, which they call the *Baha'i Faith*, will one day establish a new world order of peace and harmony that will unify all people across all nationalities, races, and religions.

The relative size and age of the religion, compared to the smaller and newer movements, merits a closer look at its mission and how its members seek to realize it. Although most of their social and ethical teachings are in harmony with western mores and outlook, it will appear that the new world order they envisage represents a merger of religion and politics which is nevertheless in tune with Islamic thinking. To understand the religion, its history, and its appeal to both believers and potential believers around the world requires some insight into Shi'i Islam in nineteenth-century Iran, which is where chapter 2 begins.

2.

The Emergence and Historical Development of the Baha'i Religion

The southeastern third of Iraq and nearly all of present-day Iran except for areas bordering Turkey constitute the heartland of Shi'i Islam, the state religion of Iran since 1501.[1] Shi'ites regard Muhammad's cousin and son-in-law Ali and his descendants through Fatima, Muhammad's daughter, as the rightful rulers of Islam. In 680 the Shi'ites lost the contest over the Muslim world to the Sunnis in a military defeat at the plain of Karbala in Iraq when Husayn, son of Ali, was killed.

Most Shi'ites acknowledge a line of eleven heredity rulers, "imams," including Ali. When the eleventh imam died in 873, his supposed son and successor mystically disappeared and was thereafter known as the Hidden Imam. Shi'ites believe he will return one day as the Mahdi ("rightly guided one") to lead his people to the day of judgment and resurrection. Millenarian expectations are thus prevalent among Shi'ites, and the Baha'is have drawn upon this legacy.

In the nineteenth century, Iran suffered unrest and economic decline in the shadow of the great powers of the day, Russia and Britain. The powerful Shi'i clergy, the "ulama," reacted in various ways to this development, some of them

associating with heterodox currents on the fringes of orthodox Shi'ism. One such development was the Shaykhi movement, named after its founder, Shaykh Ahmad Ahsa'i (1753-
1826). The Shaykhis believed that religious knowledge and
inspiration could be acquired through direct contact with
the prophet Muhammad and the imams. However, this concept was unacceptable to the majority of the ulama, and
around 1822 they broke with Shaykh Ahsa'i.

When he died in 1826, Ahsa'i was succeeded by Sayyid
Kazim Rashti (d. 1844) who, like his predecessor, was the
leader of a teaching circle in southern Iraq. This is where
Shaykhism enjoyed its greatest stronghold. Rashti taught
that a forerunner to the Hidden Imam, the "bab," or "gate,"
would soon appear. In the year 1260 AH (1843-44 CE),
there was considerable suspense because, according to the
Muslim calendar, it was one thousand lunar years since the
disappearance of the twelfth imam in 260 AH (873 CE).[2]

THE DECLARATION OF THE BAB

Sayyid Kazim Rashti died in January 1844, throwing the
Shaykhis into considerable disarray. No one was able to mo-
bilize the support necessary to become his successor. Several leading Shaykhis stepped forward only to later break
with the movement, and others began looking for a leader
outside the inner circle of Shaykhis. In May 1844 the Shaykhi Mulla Muhammad Husayn Bushru'i (1814-1849) visited the Iranian city of Shiraz and met a young merchant,
Sayyid Ali Muhammad Shirazi (1819-1850). The latter had
belonged to Rashti's teaching circle in Iraq and was acquainted with several members of the Shaykhi community.
The meeting between the two became a watershed event in
forming a revolutionary movement called Babism which
would eventually develop into modern Baha'i.

According to later Babi accounts, Mulla Husayn stayed for several days in Ali Muhammad's home to discuss different religious subjects including the issue of a successor to Rashti. During one of these discussions, Ali Muhammad asked if Mulla Husayn could not see in him, Ali Muhammad, the qualities of a successor. After several days of further, lengthy conversations and demonstrations of Ali Muhammad's skills in theological writing, Mulla Husayn became convinced. He acknowledged on the evening of 22 May 1844 Ali Muhammad's claim to be the Bab. Mulla Husayn thus became the first Babi disciple and later developed into a great Babi leader himself.

After his conversion, Mulla Husayn began lecturing and preaching in the neighboring mosque where he won several Shaykhis to the cause of the Bab. These first followers succeeded, in turn, in enrolling other new converts, mostly among Shaykhis but later also among Shi'ites in general.

THE RISE OF THE BABI MOVEMENT

In 1845, less than a year after he declared that he was the Bab, Ali Muhammad planned to go to Karbala in Iraq to await the advent of the Imam. However, the Bab chose to stay away when a religious tribunal convened in Baghdad and condemned him and one of the local Babi leaders for blasphemy. This turn of events had a devastating effect on his followers, and Babism nearly collapsed in Iraq.

In the summer of 1845, the Bab was placed under house arrest in Shiraz to avoid further unrest. Though he escaped in September 1846, he was arrested again in early 1847 and held in a fortress in northwestern Azerbaijan. Nevertheless, he was not cut off from his followers, and the Babi movement grew despite increasing opposition from the ulama. It is estimated that in the late 1840s, the total number of Babis

Iran and the Ottoman Empire in the mid-nineteenth century.

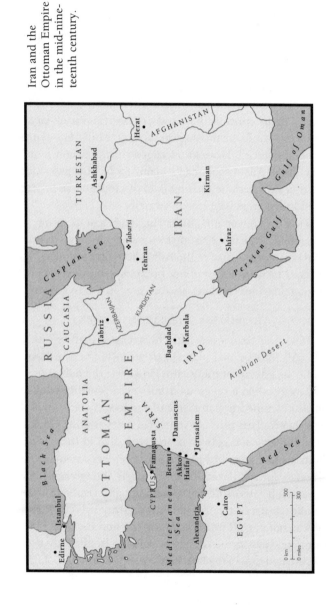

was about 100,000, or 2 percent of the Iranian population.[3]

Early in 1848 the Bab took the additional, extremely rad-ical step within Shi'ism of declaring himself to be the Hid-den Imam. Rumors of his announcement began to spread rapidly and brought the Babi movement to a crucial juncture. In the same year, the Bab wrote his most important book, the *Bayan* ("explanation"), announcing a new system of reli-gious law that would supersede Islam. It was to regulate a future Babi state that would comprise five central provinces in Iran. The Bab also engaged in numerological specula-tions, concluding that the number nineteen was particularly significant. He intended this number to become the base unit for different kinds of measurement and taxation.[4] He introduced a calendar based on the same number. The cal-endar had nineteen months, each month comprised of nine-teen days. Year one in this calendar was 1844, the year of the Bab's declaration.

Many of the Bab's prescriptions would later be abrogated in the 1870s by Baha'u'llah, who would introduce new laws.[5] However, other innovations would be retained. These in-clude various ritual practices and the calendar, which con-tinues to regulate Baha'i community life. In modern Baha'i, besides the number nineteen, the number nine is consid-ered significant.

The Bab's concept of God, which was shared by other heterodox Shi'i movements, has been retained in modern Baha'i. The religion teaches that the divine essence (God) is unknowable, indescribable, and inaccessible and that reve-lation takes place through prophets who are both divine manifestations of the Primal Will and human.[6] The Bab was one of a succession of divine revelations that began with Adam and continued through the prophets Abraham, Mo-ses, Zoroaster, Jesus, and Muhammad. The Bab was not the last of the prophets because he taught that another, "him whom God shall make manifest," would subsequently appear.[7] With this last divine manifestation, the cycle of prophecies would be fulfilled.

In July 1848 the Bab was brought to Tabriz for trial by a council of ulama and state officials under the supervision of crown prince Nasiri'd-Din Mirza. During the trial, the Bab confirmed his claim of divine authority. When the council demanded proof, he refused to satisfy them. The council therefore found him guilty of heresy. It shrank from sentencing him to death only because of his popularity.

The government began to realize after the trial what the full implications of the Bab's claims were. In Shi'i beliefs the return of the Imam meant that Islam was fulfilled and that the government should yield to its rightful ruler, the Hidden Imam returned. The authorities therefore initiated a systematic suppression of the movement that involved full-scale battles with Babi insurgents from October 1848 to the beginning of 1851. The Babis fought bravely against overwhelming odds, but they finally succumbed to the Iranian army. At least 2,000 to 3,000 Babis were killed in the campaigns and subsequent executions.[8]

The first and most important of the many battles took place in northern Iran in 1848-49 when several hundred armed Babis under the command of Mulla Husayn defended a temporary fortification created at a desolate place called Shaykh Tabarsi. After nine months of attacks and counter attacks, the starved and weakened Babis agreed to the army's terms of surrender only to be betrayed and slaughtered. For the Babis, the battles at Shaykh Tabarsi carried stark symbolism in reference to the battle at Karbala where Muhammad's grandson Husayn and his followeres had been slain.[9] In one source, Mulla Husayn is quoted: "In this place will the blood of God's soldiers and saints be shed, and many a pure spirit shall be quenched in dust and gore." Most of his companions knew what he intended to signify.[10]

This very historic scene, with besieged defenders resisting greater numbers, was of a type that can galvanize the spirit of a group or a nation. The Jewish zealots at Masada in 73 CE, the Texans at the Alamo in 1836, and the Branch Davidians' catastrophic clash with authorities at Waco, Texas, in 1993 are similar examples of dramas that deliver the material for an identity-building mythology. The historic battles of Shaykh Tabarsi play this kind of role for the Baha'is.

THE COLLAPSE OF THE BABI MOVEMENT

Not long after the Babi defeat at Shaykh Tabarsi, the government resolved to deal the Babis a death blow once and for all. It brought the Bab to Tabriz and executed him by firing squad on 9 July 1850 along with one of his disciples.[11]

Beginning in 1849 when the Bab was in prison and several of the first Babi leaders had been killed, a new generation of leaders stepped forward. Among these were the half-brothers Mirza Husayn Ali Nuri (1817-1892), later called Baha'u'llah ("Glory of God"), and Mirza Yahya Nuri (ca. 1830-1912), later called Subh-i-Azal ("Morn of Eternity"). They joined in the Babi movement early on, but unlike most other Babi leaders, they were not ulama and had not affiliated with the Shaykhi movement. Apparently Subh-i-Azal was designated to be the Bab's successor, but in the confusion following the execution of the Bab, he was unable to consolidate support as the movement became fragmented.

In August 1852 a Babi group in Tehran attempted to assassinate the shah, which prompted the retaliatory arrests of some of the Babi leaders including Baha'u'llah. Subh-i-Azal avoided being arrested by escaping to Iraq. Eventually about fifty Babi leaders were executed, some after having endured horrible torture.[12] Baha'u'llah was imprisoned in a subterranean cell in Tehran for four months, then he was exiled to Baghdad. In January 1853 he joined Subh-i-Azal and a small group of fellow Babis there.

Back in Iran, the Babis did not attempt further insurrections except for one armed upheaval in October-December 1853. In the following years, occasional individual attacks on Babis took place, mostly as isolated incidents, but periodically more systematic persecutions swept the country.

EXILE IN BAGHDAD AND
THE DECLARATION OF BAHA'U'LLAH

In Baghdad Subh-i-Azal secluded himself and left the day-to-day leadership of the Babi community to his older half-brother, Baha'u'llah. This division of responsibilities between two brothers inevitably produced some tension until Baha'u'llah decided to abandon Baghdad to live as a dervish in the Kurdistan mountains for two years (1854-56).[13] This hiatus was an important time for him, during which, and immediately afterwards he penned several significant works, which were clearly influenced by Sufi thinking.

In Baghdad the Babi community had grown considerably larger until, fearing a renewal of upheavals, the Iranian government persuaded the Ottomans to have the Babis removed from the city. In the spring of 1863, Baha'u'llah and Subh-i-Azal, with their families and a group of followers, were forcibly moved to Istanbul and later to Edirne in the European part of Turkey.

Before leaving, Baha'u'llah spent twelve days outside Baghdad in a garden called "Ridvan" ("paradise") from 21 April to 2 May 1863. Baha'i accounts tell that this is when

Baha'u'llah declared to his family and closest disciples that he was the "one whom God would make manifest" and the one whom the Bab had promised would follow as an even greater prophet than the Bab himself.[14] The days are celebrated among Baha'is as "the holiest and most significant of all Baha'i festivals."[15] However, the declaration was not openly announced until the spring of 1866 in Edirne, three years after Baha'u'llah's departure from Baghdad.[16] It resulted in an immediate split among the Babis. A minority who chose to follow Subh-i-Azal became known as Azalis, while the majority declared their allegiance to Baha'u'llah and were soon known as Baha'is, which is to say the "people of Baha" (Baha'u'llah).[17]

THE DEVELOPMENT OF THE
BAHA'I RELIGION UNDER BAHA'U'LLAH

The schism of 1866 was accented by so much unrest that in 1868 the Turkish authorities ordered the deportation of Baha'u'llah and about seventy of his followers to a remote part of the Ottoman empire, the old fortress town and Mediterranean harbor of Akko, then in Syria and now a part of Israel. Similarly, Subh-i-Azal was exiled, accompanied by his family and a few adherents, to Famagusta on the island of Cyprus, which is where he would stay until his death in 1912.

Initially Baha'u'llah and his family were imprisoned in the fortress at Akko, but in 1870 they were allowed to live in the town under observation. In 1879 they moved to a large mansion called Bahji a few miles north of Akko. There Baha'u'llah spent the rest of his life in semi-seclusion, receiving followers and the occasional visitor. When he died in 1892, he was buried in a shrine at his house, since institutionalized as the Baha'i "qiblih," or the direction members

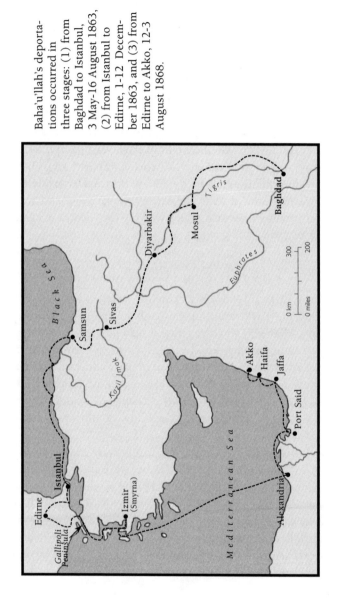

Baha'u'llah's deportations occurred in three stages: (1) from Baghdad to Istanbul, 3 May–16 August 1863, (2) from Istanbul to Edirne, 1–12 December 1863, and (3) from Edirne to Akko, 12–3 August 1868.

face when praying. It is considered by Baha'is to be the holiest place on earth.[18]

While living in the town of Akko, Baha'u'llah wrote the most central book of scripture in the Baha'i religion, the *Kitáb-i-Aqdas*. It was written around 1873, but it was not until 1992 that the first authoritative English translation was issued.[19] Until then, its contents were accessible to western Baha'is in the form of various excerpts and an edited synopsis.[20]

To some degree, Baha'u'llah's thinking reflected the liberal political trends in the west and Middle East at the time, with which he was well acquainted. However, compared to the writings of Ottoman and Persian intellectuals from the same period, Baha'u'llah was extraordinary in the religious and universal scope of his reform thinking.[21] He addressed the entire world, offering a religion that would accommodate existing traditions to a politico-religious superstructure of a unified, peaceful, prosperous world community. Many of his social teachings and views on government and international relations were transmitted through the important book, *The Secret of Divine Civilization,* written by his son Abdu'l-Baha in 1875.[22] It addresses a Persian audience and appeals for reform in Iran. It outlines a plan for the "union of the nations of the world," international law, disarmament, parliamentarism, advancement of universal education, the abolition of extreme wealth and poverty, and the useful exploitation of science and technology for the welfare of humankind. The book is critical towards traditional Iranian society, contrasting it with western modernity, which it highly praises, although the west is also criticized for its materialism and moral laxity. Most of today's Baha'i approach to social and economic issues can be traced to this work.

ABDU'L-BAHA AND EXPANSION IN THE WEST

In his will, Baha'u'llah appointed his eldest son, Abbas Effendi (1844-1921), later known as Abdu'l-Baha, to be his successor. However, Abdu'l-Baha's succession was challenged by his half-brother Muhammad-Ali, who managed to draw most of Baha'u'llah's own family and close associates away from Abdu'l-Baha. For many years, followers of Muhammad-Ali constituted a considerable local opposition although the majority of Baha'is outside Akko accepted Abdu'l-Baha.[23] Partly because of this, Abdu'l-Baha moved from Akko to nearby Haifa in 1909 and began establishing what later became the Baha'i World Centre on Mount Carmel.[24]

Abdu'l-Baha interpreted Baha'u'llah's will as a covenant between Baha'u'llah and the Baha'is.[25] Absolute commitment to Baha'u'llah's will became a central doctrine; disobedience to the covenant in which Baha'u'llah appointed Abdu'l-Baha as his successor is severely denounced. In the later schisms, the accusation of covenant breaking has been invoked as justification for the excommunication of dissidents. In reality, Baha'is have excommunicated relatively few members, but when the subject of covenant breaking is mentioned, it elicits strong feelings and gives rise to rumors.[26]

Baha'is recognize Abdu'l-Baha as the authoritative interpreter of his father's writings. In addition, Abdu'l-Baha's own works belong to the canon of sacred writ alongside those of his father and of the Bab. His views encompass themes drawn from his father's writings, but also his own statements on reformist and humanitarian issues.[27] In particular, Abdu'l-Baha must be credited for presenting Baha'i to the world in a manner that was accessible to westerners and for his success in spreading the religion far beyond its Iranian context.

The United States was a primary field for proselytizing. Ibrahim G. Kheiralla, a Baha'i of Syrian Christian background, traveled to Chicago in December 1892 and gained the first American converts there. During the subsequent years, he converted several hundred Americans from the midwest and east coast, many of them women from mainstream Protestant backgrounds who were interested in alternative religions: Theosophy, Swedenborgianism, and various Hindu traditions. Probably Baha'i was accepted as part of the trend of the age. However, Kheiralla promulgated Baha'i in a way that proved to be inconsistent with Abdu'l-Baha's interpretation of beliefs. As a result, there was a break between Kheiralla and the majority of the American Baha'is—a crisis that took several years to overcome. In 1912 Abdu'l-Baha reached out to consolidate the American Baha'i community with a celebrated eight-month tour of North America. In subsequent years the U.S. membership stabilized at between 1,000 and 2,000.[28]

Baha'i was introduced to Europe in 1898-99 by American missionaries, and Baha'i communities were established in London, Manchester, Paris, and Stuttgart. Abdu'l-Baha visited the continent three times in 1911, 1913, and 1914. In general, the proselytizing met with limited success, and the number of European Baha'is was only about one hundred at the beginning of 1913.[29]

SHOGHI EFFENDI AND
THE ROUTINIZATION OF LEADERSHIP

When Abdu'l-Baha died on 28 November 1921, his grandson Shoghi Effendi (1897-1957) became his successor, with the title of "Guardian of the Cause of God." Again the succession was challenged by Baha'u'llah's family and some of the leading western Baha'is.[30] In the process of trying to gain control over communities around the world and over property in Palestine/Israel, Shoghi Effendi ended up excommunicating all of his closest family.[31]

Shoghi Effendi proved to be a different type of leader than Abdu'l-Baha. Educated at the American University in Beirut and later Oxford University, he was fluent in English and familiar with western thinking and culture. In 1937, he married the daughter of a prominent Canadian Baha'i. He shunned the role of extroverted personal leadership in favor of organizing a bureaucracy that could cope with the demands of an expanding religion.

His assertion of authority is seen in the canonization of his organizational guidelines, "The Administrative Order of the Faith of Baha'u'llah," which are now an integral part of Baha'i doctrine. In his own words, he created an organization which was "by virtue of its origin and character, unique in the annals of the world's religious systems."[32] Baha'is consider the rules for the election of administrative bodies, for example, to be as important as the laws of prayer, fast, and personal conduct, as is evident in the wide use of a synopsis of Baha'i law and procedures, *Principles of Bahá'í Administration*.[33]

The Administrative Order established the basic unit of the religion as the "local spiritual assembly," a nine-member body elected once a year by the adult members living in a particular locality, usually within a municipality or town.[34] At the national level in each country, a nine-member assembly is annually elected by delegates to a national convention. In addition to detailing the elections and functions of these bodies, the Administrative Order gives directives in such matters as how to celebrate the "Nineteen Day Feasts" held at the beginning of each Baha'i month. The Administrative Order is, in essence, a guide for everyday life at the community level.

Aside from administrative matters, Shoghi Effendi devoted attention to expounding and promulgating select Baha'i teachings. His particular emphasis was the need for a new world order.[35] He translated parts of Baha'u'llah's writings into English, consciously selecting the style of seventeenth-century English Bible translations and thereby setting a precedent for future Baha'i translations.[36] This archaic English characterizes not only the corpus of sacred Baha'i literature but many of the periodic messages from the Baha'i World Centre as well. Doctrinally, the writings of Shoghi Effendi are not considered sacred, but his interpretations of Baha'i law are revered as authoritative and binding.[37]

A more systematic approach to proselytizing was launched in Europe after World War II. The initiative was taken by Shoghi Effendi, and the American Baha'i community was given the responsibility of coordinating the proselytizing. Virtually all the missionaries ("pioneers" and "traveling teachers") in Europe were Americans; all external administrative matters and correspondence were conducted in English. This meant that Baha'i, although of Iranian stock, gained its position in Europe as an essentially Americanized religion. The same pattern is seen for other new religions that have entered Europe by way of America rather than, for instance, directly from India.

ESTABLISHMENT OF
THE UNIVERSAL HOUSE OF JUSTICE

The situation of the international Baha'i community changed dramatically when Shoghi Effendi died on a trip to England in 1957 at only sixty years of age. He was childless, and had

not appointed a successor. The religion's leadership shifted
to a temporary nine-member committee called the Custodians, whose main task was to fulfill Abdu'l-Baha's intent,
as expressed in his will, to create a Universal House of
Justice.

As now constituted, the Universal House of Justice consists of nine men (women cannot serve), elected every fifth
year by national representatives. When convened, the Universal House of Justice is thought to be infallible in its decisions, although individually the members are not granted
any special spiritual authority beyond that of any other
member of the religion. Since 1963 the house has governed
on a wide range of matters from major policy decisions to
issues involving individuals who seek guidance through
correspondence.[38]

Some Baha'is found it difficult to adjust to the idea of collective leadership rather than one individual successor to
Shoghi Effendi.[39] One of the Custodians, a leading American Baha'i, Charles Mason Remey, announced in the spring
of 1960 that he considered himself to be the natural successor because Shoghi Effendi had appointed him president of
an advisory body, the International Baha'i Council. The
Custodians rejected his claim, so Remey independently pro-
nounced himself Guardian of Orthodox Baha'is. As in previous instances, so with this attempt to challenge the established Baha'i leadership, the only result was the formation
of yet another splinter group.[40]

Already during Shoghi Effendi's leadership, the worldwide expansion was being conducted along the lines of
long-term strategies. The Ten-Year International Baha'i Teaching and Consolidation Plan of 1953-1963 became the model
for successive plans. Since 1953, other developments include the coordination of international activities through

such auxiliaries as the Continental Boards of Counselors created in 1968, and the International Teaching Centre created in 1973. The support staff in Haifa has grown to the point that today it includes nearly eight hundred people.

The coordinated mission strategies have proved to be successful as rapid growth was achieved in many countries during the early 1970s. Baha'is grew worldwide from less than half a million in 1963 to a reported membership of more than five million by the beginning of the 1990s. The majority reside in non-western countries, as will be seen in chapter 4. In recent years the worldwide growth has been more moderate.

The elegant simplicity of the Palermo, Sicily, Baha'i center is anticipated by the street-level plaque. "Haziratu'l-Quds" is Arabic for "the sacred fold." *Photo by Margit Warburg.*

The interior of the Palermo Baha'i center. On the wall is a portrait of Abdu'l-Baha. This is typical of many Baha'i centers and private homes. *Photo by Margit Warburg.*

Abdu'l-Baha (1844-1921) established the headquarters of Baha'i on Mount Carmel in Haifa. He also initiated the expansion of Baha'i to the West. *Courtesy of the Office of Public Information, Bahá'í International Community.*

Abdu'l-Baha and Baha'i friends in Paris, 1912. Abdu'l-Baha visited Europe three times, in 1911, 1912, and 1913. *Courtesy of the Office of Public Information, Baha'i International Community.*

Shoghi Effendi (1897-1957), "Guardian of the Cause of God," an Oxford-educated administrator who oversaw the international expansion of the religion. His "Administrative Order of the Faith of Baha'u'llah" outlines how the religion is organized and its leadership elected. *Courtesy of the Office of Public Information, Baha'i International Community.*

Ruhiyyih Khanum Rabbani (1910-2000) was born Mary Sutherland Maxwell in New York City. She was married to Baha'i leader Shoghi Effendi in 1932 and lived the rest of her life in Haifa.

The author being welcomed into the Baha'i National Center in Seoul, South Korea. The religion claims a worldwide membership of about five million and a presence in 190 countries. *Photo 1991.*

The first Baha'i temple, built in 1919 in Ashkhabad, Turkestan, served a large community of Iranian emigrants. It was irreparably damaged in an earthquake in 1948 and demolished in 1963. *Courtesy of the Office of Public Information, Baha'i International Community.*

The fretwork of the spacious interior of the Baha'i temple in Wilmette, Illinois, took thirty years to complete. Baha'i temples are places of contemplation, prayer, and reading of scripture. The Sunday services usually consist of readings, chanting, and choral music. *Courtesy of Francisco González Pérez, author,* Arquitectos de Unidad.

The Baha'i temple in New Delhi is the newest and largest of seven temples worldwide and resembles the petals of a lotus flower. It attracts an average of 3.5 million visitors a year. *Courtesy of Francisco González Pérez, author, Arquitectos de Unidad.*

The well-known Baha'i landmark in the Haifa area, the Shrine of the Bab. The original square mausoleum, completed in 1909, holds the marble sarcophagus of Muhammad Ali Shirazi (1819-1850). The colonnade and dome were later additions. *Courtesy of Kevin Merrill, photographer and webmaster, "The Baha'i Holy Land."*

Baha'u'llah, founder of the Baha'i religion, died in the mansion of Bahji near Akko in 1892. His shrine is considered to be the holiest place on earth by Baha'is and indicates the direction they face in prayer. *Courtesy of the Baha'i World News Service.*

The Seat of the Universal House of Justice is situated within an expansive garden complex on Mount Carmel. This is where the highest council of the Baha'i religion meets. Elected every five years by representatives from the national spiritual assemblies, its nine members render decisions that are thought to be infallible. *Courtesy of Kevin Merrill, photographer and webmaster, "The Baha'i Holy Land."*

The International Archives Building on Mount Carmel preserves original manuscripts and artifacts, including relics of the religion and portraits of Baha'u'llah and the Bab. The dome of the Shrine of the Bab is also visible. *Courtesy of Kevin Merrill, photographer and webmaster, "The Baha'i Holy Land."*

A view of the Mediterranean coastal city of Haifa from the building known as the Centre for the Study of the Texts. Four impressive administrative buildings occupy the Baha'i World Centre garden on Mount Carmel. *Courtesy of Kevin Merrill, photographer and webmaster, "The Baha'i Holy Land."*

The author poses with a local Baha'i at the Baha'i center in Banjul, Gambia. The Baha'is run a tuition-free computer school here. *Photo 1999.*

This small shrine marks the burial place of Baha'u'llah's half-brother Mirza Yahya Nuri, better known as Subh-i-Azal ("Morn of Eternity"). He was exiled by officials of the Ottoman government to Cyprus, where he died in 1912. *Photo by Margit Warburg, 1996.*

Detail of the entrance to the Subh-i-Azal shrine on the outskirts of Famagusta, Cyprus. In the foreground is eighty-six-year-old Rida Ezel, a grandson of the founder of the Azali schism. *Photo by Margit Warburg, 1996.*

Baha'is sponsor three hundred development projects around the world including many kindergardens and elementary schools. This photo shows a class at the Ocean of Light International School in Tonga. *Courtesy of the Baha'i World News Service.*

3.

Baha'i Beliefs and Rituals

FUNDAMENTAL DOCTRINES

The Baha'i religion is strictly monotheistic. It asserts that there is one God and that the founders of the great religions such as Moses, Zoroaster, Buddha, Jesus, Muhammad, the Bab, and Baha'u'llah were all human manifestations of the same invisible, indescribable deity. According to Baha'i doctrine, the prophets contain a pure element that is inseparable from God. But the prophets are human and act as God's mouthpieces without quoting God verbatim; rather, they are influenced by their own personality, time, and cultural background.

The last and greatest manifestation of God was Baha'u'llah. This belief is fundamental to Baha'i and is what places the movement outside the realm of Islam in the eyes of both Muslims and Baha'is. It is analogous to the fundamental issue dividing Jews and Christians: the belief in Jesus as the son of God.

According to Baha'is, human beings exist in order to know and love God. People are endowed with the ability to approach God by seeking an ever-increasing understanding and love of God's attributes. It is a Baha'i principle that every human being has the right and duty to pursue truth in their own way.

Baha'is believe that each individual has a soul that continues after death to reside in a metaphorical heaven or hell. One may impact the status of a soul by praying for the dead. However, the effect of how a person lived his or her life is the important determinant of the soul's state. Baha'is reject the idea of reincarnation.

Baha'is believe in free will: a person is responsible for his or her behavior and one's fate is therefore not predetermined. Nor does the Christian idea of original sin find a place in the religion. Another significant difference between Christianity and Baha'i is that evil is not considered a principle in itself but is the absence of goodness, just as darkness is the absence of light.

Prayer and meditation are recognized paths to spiritual insight, while spiritual techniques like asceticism or self-torment are rejected. Daily prayer and reading of Baha'i scriptures are considered religious obligations.

According to Baha'is, the world's great religions represent different stages in the spiritual evolution of human society towards a unified civilization.[1] Religious and political unity are the intended consequence of the spiritual development of humankind achieved through successive revelations that culminated in the revelation of Baha'u'llah. Baha'is perceive themselves to be the vanguard of a process that will result in a new golden age for humankind, the "Most Great Peace." This will be realized when the majority of the world's people convert to Baha'i. The Most Great Peace will be preceded by a period of "Lesser Peace" when nations agree to abolish war and unite politically in response to the Baha'i call for the unification of humankind. Baha'is firmly believe that world-governing institutions can establish and perpetuate world peace. Already in 1938, for example, Shoghi Effendi wrote:

> A world federal system, ruling the whole earth and exercising unchallengeable authority over its unimaginably vast resources, blending and embodying the ideals of both the East and the West, liberated from the curse of war and its miseries, and bent on the exploitation of all the available sources of energy on the surface of the planet, a system in which Force is made the servant of Justice, whose life is sustained by its universal recognition of one God and by its allegiance to one common Revelation—such is the goal towards which humanity, impelled by the unifying forces of life, is moving.[2]

In consequence of its doctrinal support of global institutions, the Baha'i religion maintains tight relations with the United Nations. The leadership in Haifa regularly addresses the public and the world's governments with statements of Baha'i views about the world order.[3] Baha'is advocate the adoption of an international auxiliary language as well, whether newly created or selected from among the existing languages. A quotation from Baha'u'llah illustrates this praise of universalism:

> In former Epistles We have enjoined upon the Trustees of the House of Justice either to choose one language from among those now existing or to adopt a new one, and in like manner to select a common script, both of which should be taught in all the schools of the world. Thus will the earth be regarded as one country and one home. The most glorious fruit of the tree of knowledge is this exalted word: Of one tree are all ye the fruit, and of one bough the leaves.[4]

The last sentence, "Of one tree are all ye the fruit, and of one bough the leaves," is one of the most popular quotations from Baha'u'llah's writings.

Around the central doctrine of world unification, Baha'is embrace a number of social and ethical principles which reflect the liberal and reformist ideas of Baha'u'llah and Abdu'l-Baha. Baha'i doctrine condemns racial prejudice and stresses equal rights and opportunities for men and women. Baha'is insist on compulsory education and the elimination of extreme poverty and wealth. The Baha'i doctrines are often referred to as the "twelve principles," encompassing the basic teachings of Baha'u'llah. Unlike, say, the Ten Commandments, the twelve principles are not fixed with respect to their exact wording or to the order in which they are listed. They are:

> Oneness of mankind.
> Independent investigation of truth.
> Common foundation of all religions.
> Oneness of religion.
> Essential harmony of science and religion.
> Equality of men and women.
> Elimination of the extremes of wealth and poverty.
> Elimination of prejudice of all kinds.
> Universal compulsory education.
> A spiritual solution to economic problems.
> A universal auxiliary language.
> Universal peace upheld by a world government.

The religion's ethos is therefore primarily this-worldly and collective, remaining true to its origins in Islamic millennialism. In accordance with its non-Christian background, the religion is not overly concerned with individual salvation, either here or in the hereafter. In their personal lives,

Baha'is work in secular professions and observe the general moral codes of society. Baha'i law forbids believers to drink alcohol or to take drugs. It prescribes a yearly fasting period. Baha'is have otherwise not retained the dietary prohibitions of Islam.

THE BAHA'I YEAR

The nineteen-day, nineteen-month calendar was devised by the Bab, as previously discussed. The names of the months are derived from a Shi'i dawn prayer recited during the Muslim month of Ramadan.[5] The days one through nineteen are called by the same names as the corresponding months: thus, the fourth day is called *Azamat* just as the fourth month. A new day begins at sunset as is the custom for Muslim and Jewish calendars.

Unlike the Muslim calendar, which is strictly lunar, Baha'i reckoning is solar-based, as is the traditional Persian calendar. Since nineteen times nineteen is 361, there are missing days that have to be added each year to complete the solar count of 365 or, in the case of leap years, 366 days. These four or five intercalary days, known as the Ayyam-i-Ha, are inserted between the eighteenth and nineteenth months. The ancient Zoroastrian New Year, called Naw-Ruz, is celebrated on the vernal equinox, 21 March. Since this is the Iranian national New Year and is celebrated by all Iranians, it is not uniquely Baha'i.

The calendar notes holy days such as the twelve-day period of Ridvan commemorating Baha'u'llah's declaration as a Manifestation of God. The first, ninth, and twelfth days of Ridvan are particularly important. Other major holidays are the Declaration of the Bab and the birth and death dates of the Bab and Baha'u'llah. Altogether, including Naw-Ruz, this makes nine major holidays that are obligatory for all

Baha'is to observe by suspending work. There are also two
minor holidays that commemorate Abdu'l-Baha's death and
the Day of the Covenant; it is permitted to work on these
days. The intercalary Ayyam-i-Ha are not holidays, but Baha'u'llah gave instructions that, during this time, Baha'is
should "provide good cheer for themselves, their kindred
and, beyond them, the poor and needy. ..."[6] In modern
Baha'i communities, Ayyam-i-Ha has developed into an annual children's festival.

The figure opposite gives an overview of the Baha'i calendar. The nineteen-day months and four intercalary days are
represented by the inner circle; the outer rim represents the
Gregorian calendar. Notice that February is represented by
a slightly smaller arc than March and that differences of one
day can be distinguished. Note that the month Sharaf begins
on 31 December, or rather, the evening of 30 December to
be precise.

BAHA'I FESTIVALS

There are additional special days of communal feasts and
commemorations on the Baha'i calendar. In fact, the Nineteen Day Feast that is held on the first day of each month is
the backbone of Baha'i religious life. It developed from a
tradition of meeting together for a common meal and devo-
tion that was established by Abdu'l Baha. American Baha'is
have observed the Nineteen Day Feasts since around 1905.[7]
Shoghi Effendi institutionalized its present form to consist
of three parts: a devotional session, followed by an administrative part, and finally a social gathering.[8] Only Baha'is
are allowed to participate, whereas other Baha'i festivals
are welcoming of non-Baha'i visitors.

A Nineteen Day Feast is usually hosted by a member of a
local spiritual assembly, most often in the person's home.

Individuals may also celebrate the feast outside of a formal assembly where a group has less than nine members. When traveling, Baha'is often attend feasts in other locales.[9] Indeed, observance of the feast is viewed as a key measure of the health of a local Baha'i community.[10]

A typical feast begins in the evening with readings from

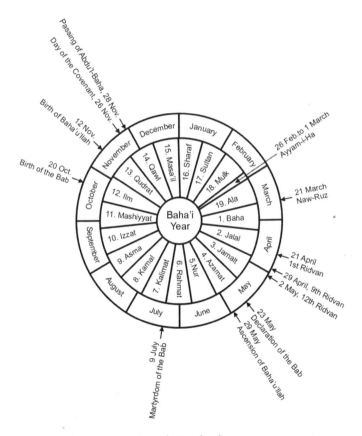

The Baha'i Calendar

the sacred writings. Usually the host has decided who should read what. The assembly's secretary provides some general information and news on Baha'i matters, after which the treasurer gives an account of the assembly's financial situation. The meeting continues with the exchange of greetings and perhaps some talk about recent news or an upcoming event. Before tea and cookies, which mark the end of the evening, one or two members might conduct a discussion about how to promote the faith or some other topic of general importance.

My studies indicate that in small European Baha'i communities, commitment to these monthly gatherings is strong. A majority of Danish Baha'is have hosted a Nineteen Day Feast at least once during the year and say that they otherwise attended most of them. Those who did not participate often lived far from the nearest local spiritual assembly as isolated Baha'is.

Like the Nineteen Day Feast, holidays are usually celebrated communally with a program that might be held in a local Baha'i center for about thirty or more participants. There is often a session of prayer and chanting (a melodious prayer performed in Arabic or Persian), one or two speeches on a topic related to the particular event, and some entertainment. The program usually ends with tea and cakes or even a complete meal, often with Iranian dishes.

The holidays are social, joyous occasions. Below is an example from my notes for a feast held in Copenhagen in 1990. In this case, it was the celebration of the Birth of Baha'u'llah which begins on the evening of 11 November:

- Welcome.
- Reading from Baha'i scriptures in the vernacular

(Danish), English, and in Persian and Arabic. Chanting of prayers in Persian.

- A speech by an Iranian Baha'i on the legends of the births of all the great prophets from Moses to Baha'u'llah.
- A speech by a western Baha'i on how the religion has progressed since the days of Baha'u'llah.
- A dramatization by four young Baha'is. The primary character is a poker-faced detective in a fedora, looking distinctly like Phillip Marlowe. His assignment is to find the gate to God and the reward of eternal life. He goes to a number of places and meets a Muslim mullah (a slight caricature), an attractive young woman at a hamburger stand, and a lady in a bookshop who ends up giving him *Selections from the Writings of the Báb*.
- A religious song by a group of children, both boys and girls of different ethnic backgrounds.
- Tea and an abundance of cakes of various sorts.

The holy days associated with the deaths of the Bab, Baha'u'llah, and Abdu'l-Baha are celebrated with programs that are similar to this but more somber. Naw-Ruz is celebrated as a New Year's Eve party. People dress up, Baha'u'llah's Naw-Ruz message is read, and there may be music and fireworks. The selection of cakes is even richer than usual.

Baha'is have other feasts and celebrations. United Nations Day (24 October) is often celebrated with public invitations to non-Baha'is. The main event might be a lecture or perhaps a film, followed by socializing with, of course, Persian food or cakes, tea, and coffee. The day seems to have turned into something of a secular holiday much like the various national independence or constitutional days for citizens in general.

RITUALS

The two most fundamental religious observances in Baha'i are the daily prayer and the yearly fast. In the *Kitáb-i-Aqdas* the prescriptions for prayer and fasting follow immediately the five introductory verses containing the confession of faith in Baha'u'llah as the "Dayspring of His Revelation and the Fountain of His Laws" and the command to abide God's laws.[11] In Shoghi Effendi's words, prayer and fasting constitute "the two pillars that sustain the revealed Law of God," the observance of which are "a spiritual and vital obligation enjoined by Bahá'u'lláh upon every believer who has attained the age of fifteen."[12] The doctrinal prominence of these observances makes them potentially constitutive of Baha'i identity.

Prayer

The prescribed forms for daily prayer are clearly Islamic.[13] For example, petitioners wash their hands and faces prior to praying and face the direction of the qiblih, Baha'u'llah's shrine at Bahji, just as Muslims face toward Mecca.[14] However, Baha'is are prohibited from gathering for daily communal prayer as Muslims do.[15]

There are three types of invocations: a short prayer to be said at noon; a somewhat longer prayer said in the morning, afternoon, and evening; and a long prayer to be said once in a twenty-four hour period.[16] According to Shoghi Effendi, members are free to choose any one of the three forms, but they must follow the accompanying prescriptions with respect to time and appropriate ablutions.[17]

In my study of the Danish Baha'i community in the 1980s, I found that the great majority (78 percent) observed prayer regularly, although not always daily. Twelve percent prayed less regularly. Only 5 percent reported that they never prayed, and they consisted of those who were inactive; for example, they also rarely or never attended feasts or other meetings arranged by the local group. Some of them later resigned. This indicates that if a Baha'i does not pray, he or she has begun to disengage from the religion. I found that, in general, women obey the daily observance more than men, but I found no difference between Iranians, Danes, or other national groups. The high prevalence of regular praying among all national groups is in contrast to the much more complicated picture in the case of the fast.

Fast

During the nineteen days of Ala, which is the month of fast, Baha'is are expected to abstain from food, drink, and tobacco every day from sunrise to sunset.[18] The tradition is basically the same for Muslims during Ramadan, and it should be noted that in Iran it is normal to fast for a month. For westerners, the prescribed fast is something less familiar. This is not a trivial issue, the tradition being embedded as it is in a complex cultural background. Baha'i law stipulates that all but those who are exempted are required to fast, the exceptions being children and those over seventy years of age, the sick, travelers, and women while menstruating, pregnant, or nursing. People who are engaged in heavy physical labor are exempted but are advised to eat "with frugality and in private."[19]

In my interviews in Denmark, I found that the tradition is difficult for many native Danes to live up to. With one exception, all of the Iranian Baha'is in Denmark fasted, although not always for the entire period, compared to only a little more than half (54 percent) of the Danes. Those of other nationalities fell in between these two benchmarks.

From comments I received, it appears that Iranians accepted the fast in principle and those who gave it up did so because of personal discomfort. In contrast, some Danes see it as a matter of choice—something they deliberately choose to follow or not even though they are active participants in all other aspects of their religion. Some of the reasons they gave were:

> I derive no spiritual or physical benefits.
>
> I live an austere life; I do not need the ecstasy, nor am I attracted to it. I do not want to go wild.
>
> I practice other forms of self-control. I do not smoke, and I buy as little as possible.
>
> I am against fasting when I have to engage in physical labor. You can cut down on material things instead.

In other words, these Danes interpreted the fast according to how it might benefit them or as a general period of continence, a time of reduced reliance on material goods, for instance. This innovative interpretation may have been derived from the following guideline:

> The fasting period, which lasts nineteen days, starting as a rule from the second of March every year and ending on the twentieth of the same month, involves complete abstention from food and drink from sunrise till sunset. It is essentially a period of meditation and prayer, of spiritual recuperation, during which the believer must strive to make the necessary readjustments in his inner life, and to refresh and reinvigorate the spiritual forces latent in his soul. Its significance and purpose are, therefore, fundamentally spiritual in character. Fasting is symbolic, and a reminder of abstinence from selfish and carnal desires.[20]

In the above quotation, Shoghi Effendi says that the fast is "a reminder of abstinence," and some of the Danish Baha'is transform this statement's prescription of proper observance into one of several possible means to learn "abstinence from selfish and carnal desires." By contrast, the Iranians do not interpret the ordinance in that way, but accept it as a religious duty. A comment from one of them is illustrative: "I fast because Baha'u'llah has said so." He had no doubt that the fast was obligatory rather than merely a recommended way of learning abstinence.

The different attitudes illustrate how subcultures can exist even within such a small religious community as the Danish Baha'is. There are other significant differences in attitudes and behavior, especially between Iranians and westerners. To be a Baha'i is an important part of a member's identity, but national background is also a significant component.

Collective Rites

Baha'is have few prescribed collective rituals: a brief wedding vow, spoken aloud, and a communal prayer for the dead. They otherwise generally discourage formal rituals.[21] They may, upon meeting, greet each other by saying, "Allah-u-Abha" (God is most glorious). There are few other formalities connected with Baha'i social life.

The weddings involve a short ceremony with a vow that is said in the presence of witnesses: "We will all, verily, abide by the will of God." The ceremony has to be authorized by the local spiritual assembly, which sees to it that the parents have consented to the marriage. Although such consent is required, young people choose their own partners, arranged marriages having no foundation in Baha'i law. A Baha'i can freely marry either a fellow-Baha'i or a non-Baha'i and as long as the couple has a Baha'i ceremony, they may also be married by civil authorities or by a Christian priest, for example.

Baha'i teachings enjoin chastity before marriage. For married couples, there are no prohibitions against the use of contraception. In principle, abortion is permitted for medical reasons only; in practice, no restrictions are imposed. Divorce is permitted but discouraged. Baha'u'llah prescribed a "year of waiting" before a divorce can be finalized, during which time a couple consults with the local assembly and makes an attempt at reconciliation.[22]

The funeral rite is more elaborate and has remained essentially unchanged from the original form prescribed by the Bab. According to the tradition, the body is washed and then wrapped in five pieces of white silk or cotton. A ring is placed on the finger with the inscription: "I came forth from God, and return unto Him, detached from all save Him, holding fast to His Name, the Merciful, the Compassionate."[23] The body is placed in a coffin and buried with its feet facing the qiblih. Cremation is forbidden.

A prayer for the dead is recited by one person on behalf of all present. Everyone in the congregation stands for the six-verse prayer. It begins with a short prologue written by Baha'u'llah. The greeting "Allah-u-Abha" is said, followed by the first verse which is repeated nineteen times. The next verses are said likewise, beginning with "Allah-u-Abha" and repeated nineteen times. After the prayer, there may be a reading from Baha'i writings or sometimes singing or a speech.

The burial must take place as soon as possible after the death and within an hour's journey from where the person died. Thus, when Shoghi Effendi died suddenly in London, he was buried at the New Southgate Cemetery. Baha'is subsequently purchased the area around the grave and today people can go there and pay their respects. Iranian Baha'is especially make this a travel destination.[24] In some countries, but particularly in Iran and Israel, Baha'is have their own graveyards. In other areas of the world, they are mostly buried in public cemeteries.

Another expectation of adult Baha'is is that they draft a will. Among western Baha'is, this is recognized as a duty but is nevertheless not granted a high priority. According to the *Kitáb-i-Aqdas,* the deceased's property should be divided into 2,520 shares and distributed to the family and others in specified proportions. National civil law usually prevents these Baha'i laws from taking effect.

As previously explained, the religion has no priesthood, and the absence of functionaries, as well as the scarcity of collective rituals and the relative priority of social and economic teachings, is considered unusual in western societies that are accustomed to Christian churches.

PILGRIMAGE

Baha'u'llah received visitors throughout his life in Baghdad, Edirne, Akko, and Bahji, and these visits evolved into the present Baha'i pilgrimage to the Haifa area. A pilgrimage is a much desired experience for many Baha'is who often wait years before being allowed to go. At present about three thousand Baha'is make pilgrimages each year in groups of 150, which is about the maximum that can be accommodated within the program.

The pilgrimage program lasts for nine days, starting every second Monday during the pilgrimage season from the end of October to the end of July.[25] The pilgrims stay in local hotels and are taken to the holy places on busses by guides who speak English, Farsi, French, and German. The pilgrims visit and pray at the shrines of Baha'u'llah and the Bab and are shown the buildings and monuments of the Baha'i World Centre. At the International Archives, they are shown portraits of Baha'u'llah and the Bab. This is an extraordinary experience, in part because it is forbidden to display these images at any other time. The pilgrims also visit the many places in and around Akko and surroundings which are connected with the lives of Baha'u'llah and Abdu'l-Baha. In the evenings they gather at the Pilgrim House for speeches by members of the Universal House of Justice and the International Teaching Centre. Younger staff at the World Centre often attend these events to socialize with the visitors.

One of the highlights of the trip is the Pilgrimage Tea on the second day, after the group has paid a visit to the Shrine of Baha'u'llah in the morning. They gather at 3:30 p.m. in the central reception hall of the Seat of the Universal House of Justice and socialize for a half hour over tea. The tables are then cleared and the staff leave the room. At 4:00 all the members of the House of Justice arrive. Opening prayers are offered in English and in Persian. A housemember welcomes them and talks about the significance of a pilgrimage. After a closing prayer, housemembers mingle with the crowd and the entire ceremony is over by 5:00.

On the last evening, the pilgrims gather again in the Pilgrim House, but this time not to listen to an address. Housemembers and their wives, members of the International Teaching Centre and their spouses, and many of the staff mingle with the visitors. Adjacent to the Pilgrim House is the illuminated Shrine of the Bab. On this special evening, the shrine is opened on two sides so that the vault with the sarcophagus of Abdu'l-Baha can be visited. This otherwise occurs only on the holy days. The guests approach the shrine, take off their shoes, and pray as one of the house-members chants or recites a prayer.

The pilgrimage offers an important opportunity to spread Baha'i ideas, manners, and cultural innovations, both to and from the Baha'i World Centre and among the pilgrims themselves. During the pilgrimage, people who have not known each other before experience and share part of the official Baha'i culture with which they all identify.

BAHA'I SYMBOLS

There are two symbols that are often used by Baha'is. One is "the Greatest Name," a calligraphied Arabic form of the word *baha,* meaning glory—the most sacred symbol in Baha'i. It is prominently displayed in the temples, in Baha'i centers, and in many Baha'i homes.

The Greatest Name

The ringstone symbol

The second, the so-called ringstone symbol, was designed by Abdu'l Baha. It consists of three horizontal strokes which represent the world of God, the manifestation or will (of God), and the world of man. A vertical line crossing the horizontal strokes depicts the manifestation who joins God and mankind. Two stars flanking the central figure represent the Bab and Baha'u'llah.[26] The symbol is engraved on finger rings and on other jewelry worn by Baha'is.

Baha'i is also often represented by a nine-pointed star, and this symbol is widely employed in Baha'i illustrations

and art. It often appears on the headstones of Baha'i graves
where it is forbidden to use the Greatest Name or the ringstone symbol.[27]

ECONOMIC RITUALS

Baha'is do not have a fixed fee that is required for membership privileges. Donations are confidential and voluntary.
Assemblies are not allowed to accept financial aid from
non-Baha'is except that they seek the same tax exemption
afforded other religious communities in most countries.

The Baha'is have developed the collection of money into
a semi-ritual practice because the donations are not only
seen as an economic issue but also as a religious duty and an
act of religious significance.[28] Shoghi Effendi emphasized
this:

> Not the amount you give, but the very act of doing your part
> to ensure an ample supply of "life-blood" to the body of the
> Cause, is the important thing. No individual is functioning
> as a full member of the World Order of Bahá'u'lláh who does
> not support the Fund, however modestly.[29]

Therefore, to give money is something that every adherent
needs to do in order to consider himself or herself a Baha'i.
The exclusion of non-Baha'is who are not allowed to donate
adds to the sense of community identity.

The collection proceeds as a part of the Nineteen Day
Feast where non-Baha'is are excluded. Participants are not
to disclose the amount of money they give, for example, by
bringing it to the feast in an envelope. At the appointed
time, the treasurer collects the donations. Neither the names
of the donors nor the individual amounts are given; only the
total sum is announced to the group. The emphasis is therefore on the collective character of the collection.

Baha'is also transfer money to specified accounts that are administered by the national spiritual assembly, whereby it is common to earmark contributions for specific causes. Bahai's are encouraged to contribute to such projects as the maintenance of the World Centre, aid to new communities in Eastern Europe, or a new fax machine at a national center.

HUQUQU'LLAH

There is another, specialized form of contribution known as Huququ'llah, which is a self-imposed, percentage-based tax. It is more complicated than tithing (10 percent) but still bears a relationship to the percentage-based assessments common to some religious communities. Baha'u'llah made the Huququ'llah compulsory, but the payment was slowly implemented and it was only observed by Iranian Baha'is. Despite the prestige that was bestowed on practitioners, the Universal House of Justice only decided in 1984 that the time was ripe to introduce the system to all Baha'is. It has since been gradually implemented worldwide.

Huququ'llah means "the right of God" and is paid via a local trustee to the Huququ'llah fund at the World Centre. The main principle is that an individual should contribute part of his or her annual profit. The individual first deducts from a year's income what is thought necessary to live, including such assets as housing and certain business expenses. Huququ'llah is due if the remaining liquid assets have a value above nineteen *mithquals* of gold. This is equal to 69.2 grams (2.44 oz.), roughly the value of $850. Nineteen percent of this is paid as Huququ'llah, and the payment is rounded down to a whole unit of nineteen mithquals. That the holy number nineteen is the basis for the calculation demonstrates the sacred nature of the donation.

4.

Baha'is in the World

Members of the Baha'i religion are not particularly visible in western societies. Because they do not dress
differently and are not aggressive, although eager, in their
proselytizing, they tend to blend into the background of
western pluralism. Baha'i centers are often ordinary houses
or apartments situated in middle-class or upper-middle-
class neighborhoods, and only on close inspection would
one notice a nameplate announcing their presence. This
relative invisibility means that Baha'is are much less known
than other religious groups with far fewer members. For
example, British sociologist Eileen Barker found that in
1978 there were only 517 members of the Unification
Church ("Moonies") in Britain and noted, "It is under-
standable that people confuse visibility with quantity."[1] At
the same time, there were 3,182 registered Baha'is in England alone, but the amount of publicity they received was
insignificant.[2]

THE NUMBER AND
DISTRIBUTION OF BAHA'IS WORLDWIDE

According to official Baha'i sources, there are currently about
five million adherents around the world. Each year national
Baha'i communities submit reports about membership sta-

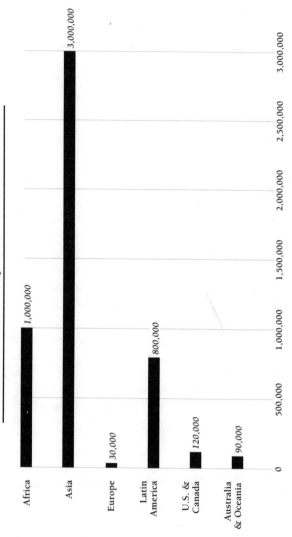

Estimated World Baha'i Population 1999. Total: 5 Million

Africa — 1,000,000

Asia — 3,000,000

Europe — 30,000

Latin America — 800,000

U.S. & Canada — 120,000

Australia & Oceania — 90,000

tus, the formation of local spiritual assemblies, the exchange of missionaries, translation of literature, and other statistical information to the Baha'i World Centre. This allows personnel to assemble detailed statistical information about the religion's patterns of expansion. Of course, the validity depends on the quality of data submitted, but there is reason to believe that, at least in the European communities, the data are reliable.

Key statistics on growth, as measured by the number of local spiritual assemblies and the number of countries and territories where Baha'is reside, are released regularly in a series of yearbooks, *The Bahá'í World.* Baha'is maintain that they are the "second most widespread of the independent world religions" with a presence in 190 countries and a total of nearly 16,000 local spiritual assemblies.[3] This is an impressive number, although it should be acknowledged that the membership is spread rather thinly in some areas. Baha'is often relocate on direction of a national spiritual assembly to meet the requirement of nine adult members in a particular locale.[4] Consequently, many assemblies consist of just nine or a few more members and are vulnerable to slight fluctuations.

The number of adherents who actively participate in the community is smaller than the above-mentioned five million. Entry into Baha'i involves signing a printed card affirming one's belief in Baha'u'llah as the Manifestation of God. The number of new converts can therefore be counted with reasonable accuracy. But as in any lay organization, some members are more active than others. Passive Baha'is are not expelled simply due to their inactivity in community life since, in principle, they could still be believing Baha'is. The fact that there is no fixed membership subscription means that lapsed members have no economic motive to resign their affiliation. In Europe the proportion of inactive members is probably not more than 10-20 percent judging from my investigations of Danish assemblies.[5] However, in areas such as the United States, 30-40 percent has had no contact with the organization for years, even though they are still counted.[6]

The typical assembly in western communities is ethnically diverse. Half or more of the European members are native to the country where they reside, while Iranian immigrants make up 25 to 40 percent. The rest are from other countries, increasingly from non-western areas. Apart from the ethnic composition, the groups match the general population with respect to gender, age distribution, and family structure. However, they tend to be above average in education and social class.

On the basis of the statistical material available from the Baha'i World Centre, the number of registered Baha'is on each continent can be estimated as shown below. Europeans comprise less than 1 percent of the total membership. Western Baha'is in general make up only 3 percent of the total five million. It should be noted that the figures include a certain proportion of members who are inactive but who have not formally resigned.

BAHA'I TEMPLES

Baha'i houses of worship, or temples, are conspicuous tokens of the religion's presence in seven cities throughout the world. The temples are envisaged as the nuclei of entire, self-contained communities that in the future will include social and educational institutions. A temple complex with its accessory institutions is referred to as a *Mashriqu'l-Adhkar* (dawning-place of the remembrance of God). The underlying concept is that these complexes should be locations where there is direct and constant interaction between spiritual and secular activities.[7] The hope is that one day these will constitute the "foundation for a new and higher type of human association."[8] At present, only one of the temples has had a social institution associated with it, the Baha'i Home for the Aged, close to the temple in Wilmette, Illinois, which functioned from 1958 to 2001.[9]

The temples conform to the same symmetrical, nine-sided plan with a large central room and an overarching dome. There are nine entrances and other symmetrical details based on the number nine. Natural light filters into the hall through windows and openings in the dome. The calligraphy of the Greatest Name is placed in the apex of the dome or in an equally conspicuous location. The interior and exterior surfaces may be ornamented with abstract frets and Arabesque borders in light stucco, and there may be additional decorations including calligraphied plaques, although pictures and statues are forbidden. Aside from the human voice, no musical instruments are allowed in the temples. The central room is furnished with chairs arranged in lecture hall fashion. It is clear that the design is inspired by the classical mosque, but Baha'i temples have their own unique and remarkable style. Several of them have become popular tourist attractions.

The first temple was built in Ashkhabad, Turkmenistan (then Russian Turkestan), in the opening years of the twentieth century. It served as the hub of a flourishing community of Iranian refugees who settled there in the 1880s.[10] After the Russian Revolution, conditions deteriorated. The temple was expropriated by the Soviet government, as with other religious property, and was converted over to secular use in 1928. In 1948 it was damaged in an earthquake and subsequently demolished in 1963.[11]

The design was based on instructions from Abdu'l-Baha, and it in turn became the inspiration for a second temple built on the shores of Lake Michigan in Wilmette, a suburb of Chicago, which was begun in the 1920s and completed in 1953. This spectacular enneagonal building is a unique mixture of oriental and western architectural styles.

Six more Baha'i temples have been completed since World War II in Kampala (Uganda), Langenhain near Frankfurt am Main (Germany), Sydney, (Australia), Apia (West Samoa), Panama City (Panama), and New Delhi (India). The New Delhi temple is the newest and largest with a diameter of 230 feet and a height of 135 feet. The dome is particularly striking, its curved, interlacing concrete shells forming the shape of a lotus flower. Since its completion in 1986, it has been a major tourist attraction.

The Baha'i temples are open to the public. Lectures and common devotional sessions are held in the temples on a regular basis. I attended the Mashriqu'l-Adhkar of Langenhain on a Sunday afternoon on 1 May 1994 and observed a typical service. It was held at 3:00 p.m. and lasted about a half-hour. Sixty-three people attended, of which one-third were Iranians. Nine people on the front row performed the service. They rose one by one and went to the speaker's chair where they addressed the audience. They were both Iranian and European and included men and women. They read from Baha'i texts, the Bhagavad-gita, the New Testament, and the Qu'ran. Most of the passages were read aloud in German or Persian, once in French, and some were chanted in Persian or Arabic.[12] The universalist tenor of the service was apparent from the inclusion of so many religions, languages, and nationalities.

The temples are conspicuous, imposing symbols of the Baha'i religion besides being houses of worship for Baha'is.

They have been intentionally distributed one per continent to symbolize the Baha'i presence around the world. As yet, no one has made a thorough study of the temples' architecture and use, but such a study would probably offer interesting perspectives on the Baha'i religion and its adherents.

THE SHRINE OF THE BAB
AND THE BAHA'I WORLD CENTRE

The one place in the world where a Baha'i presence is more salient than at the temple sites is in Haifa where the Shrine of the Bab with its golden dome is the most prominent landmark in the city. It is one of several remarkable buildings that comprise the Baha'i World Centre. The total estate, including locations in Haifa, Akko, and vicinity, consists of 129 acres.

For over a hundred years, extending back to 1891, the Baha'i World Centre has been the hub of Baha'i history. According to Baha'i sources, Baha'u'llah and Abdu'l-Baha once traveled to Haifa from Bahji to climb the slopes of Mount Carmel. From an elevated spot, Baha'u'llah pointed out a location farther down the slope "which was to serve as the permanent resting place of the Bab, and on which a befitting mausoleum was later to be erected."[13] A cluster of tall cypresses visible behind the shrine is said to be where the two men stood. Abdu'l-Baha negotiated with the Mount Carmel landowners and instructed Iranian Baha'is to transfer the Bab's remains from Tehran to Haifa. The casket arrived on 31 January 1899. That same year the foundation stone was laid for the square mausoleum with nine rooms. When the first six rooms were finished in 1909, the marble sarcophagus containing the casket was placed in the vault.

Shoghi Effendi expanded the mausoleum to include a colonnade around the original structure and an octagonal

superstructure on top, crowned by a golden dome. He continued to buy land in Haifa to expand the property beyond
the shrine and upwards. The steep slope has since been par-
tially leveled into a wide arc to accommodate other buildings that today constitute the administrative hub of the
Baha'i World Centre.

Shoghi Effendi supervised preparation of the surrounding gardens which so distinctively blend eastern and western
styles. An unexpected feature of the gardens for westerners
is that there are no benches or other places to sit and enjoy
the beauty of the surroundings, but the landscaping was intended to facilitate contemplative strolls.

The Symbolism of the Shrine of the Bab

Abdu'l-Baha executed a symbol-laden and powerful plan
when he designed and built the shrine. Its location, far
from being on just any hill, is on a mountain that is revered
by Jews, Christians, and Muslims alike. It is where the
prophet Elijah is said to have dwelt in a cave not far from
the site of the shrine. The mountain is praised several times
in Baha'u'llah's writings, notably in the *Tablet of Carmel*.[14]
Furthermore, by successfully claiming the remains of the
Bab, Abdu'l-Baha effectively demonstrated to opponents
his rightful monopoly of the Bab's legacy.

For Baha'is the Bab's remains are the center of a sacred
geography with nine concentric circles. The outermost circle is the entire world and the innermost circle surrounds
the sarcophagus containing "that inestimable Jewel, the
Báb's Holy Dust," which is considered so precious that, according to Abdu'l-Baha, the very earth surrounding the
shrine is endowed with religious potency.[15] Portions of the
shrine are open to the public in the morning, but other

areas, such as the vault with Abdu'l-Baha's sarcophagus, are accessible only to Baha'is.

A flight of stairs descends from the shrine to the foot of Mount Carmel with nine richly decorated terraces. Another flight of stairs ascends above the shrine, also with nine terraces. Including the platform of the shrine itself, the number of terraces is nineteen in all (9+9+1).[16] That the architecture is based on these numbers indicates the religious significance of these stairs. This goes back to Abdu'l-Baha who saw in a vision that the kings of the earth would one day walk up the staircase as pilgrims carrying bouquets of flowers.[17]

The Administrative Buildings of the Baha'i World Centre

The dominant building of the upper garden is the Seat of the Universal House of Justice, a neoclassical, three storied, rectangular building with a long colonnade and a central dome. The bright, bluish-green tiles of the roof stand out in sharp contrast to the shining white marble of the pillars and walls. The building is the centerpiece of the administrative buildings of the arc: the International Archives Building, the International Teaching Centre, the Centre for the Study of the Texts, and the future International Baha'i Library.

The International Archives Building is in the style of a Greek temple. It was the first structure to be erected in the arc and has a dual purpose as both a museum and a place of pilgrimage. This is where precious relics of Baha'i are preserved: the garments of the Bab, samples of Baha'u'llah's hair and blood, the sword of the famous Babi leader Mulla Husayn, and various original manuscripts.[18] Already mentioned are the portraits of Baha'u'llah and the Bab which are otherwise never shown—only to the pilgrims when they visit the archives.[19]

The Special Position of the Baha'i World Centre

The Baha'i World Centre is more than a headquarters staffed by professionals, it is also looked to as a confirmation of faith. Baha'is envisage these buildings as the seat of a future world government, the divine kingdom on earth that will unite all mankind under the religious and political banner of Baha'i. In other words, the buildings are not temporary. When the Seat of the Universal House of Justice was built, it was constructed of the same marble used for the Acropolis in Athens because "the Parthenon has retained its beauty for twenty-five centuries."[20] It is clear that the Bahai's have invested a substantial amount of money in the Mount Carmel complex. According to my calculations, the national Baha'i communities around the world must send close to one-third of all the money they collect to fund the building projects on Mount Carmel.[21]

The Baha'i World Centre is, in fact, a most remarkable religious metropolis. The extensive communication with Baha'is throughout the world, the pilgrims and other visitors from all corners of the earth, the enormous prestige of the site, the international atmosphere, the historical and religious sentiments connected with its holy places, and the absolute authority of the Universal House of Justice all prompt one to think of the Vatican in Rome or the Mormon headquarters in Salt Lake City.

The relationship between the state of Israel and Baha'is is another indication of the special position of the Baha'i World Centre. Israel is the only country in the world where Baha'is have decided that no national Baha'i community may be formed for the time being; there are no Israeli Baha'is, at least not in Israel, and no Baha'i missionaries in the country. The staff at the Baha'i World Centre do not elect a spiritual assembly and do not celebrate Nineteen Day Feasts. This underscores the status of the Baha'i World Centre as a capital city standing apart from the communities it serves. From Mount Carmel, the signal that is communicated is that this is a global religion with all local Baha'i communities on equal footing and all looking to Haifa for direction.

BAHA'I MISSION STRATEGIES

Baha'is are encouraged to engage in proselytizing activities. In the smaller, well-knit Baha'i communities, the majority of members are active in telling family, friends, and colleagues about their religion. This individual approach, through Baha'is' own interpersonal networks, is the most significant avenue of recruitment in Europe and North America. However, in some third-world countries and parts of the U.S. rural south, there have occasionally been mass conversions.

Baha'i communities generally do not have vast economic resources for missions. This reality is reflected in the choice of mission methods. Some outreach activities take the form of staged events in public places. Meetings and exhibitions at libraries and other public institutions are fairly common. In some cities Baha'is rent a small shop and use the storefront window for display. Street missions are rarely applied in the form typified by ISKCON (Hare Krishna), for example, although Baha'is have occasionally circulated pamphlets in the streets.

Missionaries

Proselytizing religions send out missionaries, and Baha'is are no exception. On the contrary, many of them are called to relocate for long or short periods either within their home countries or to foreign lands to assist local Baha'i communities in mission work. This is called "pioneering" and the missionaries "pioneers."

The Baha'i World Centre coordinates the international

Mission Statistics (Pioneering) for the Seven Year Plan, 1979-1986

	AFRICA	AMERICAS	ASIA	AUSTRALASIA	EUROPE	Total
Number of pioneers:						
Sent	159	1370	1544	130	491	3,694
Received	746	980	671	256	1,041	3,694
Difference	-587	+390	+873	-126	-550	0
Number of Baha'is:						
By 1979	603,000	665,000	2,264,000	70,000	19,000	3,621,000
By 1986	969,000	857,000	2,807,000	84,000	22,000	4,739,000
Percent Increase	61%	29%	24%	20%	16%	31%

^aBased upon data from the *Seven Year Plan, 1979-1986: Statistical Report* (Haifa: [Baha'i World Centre], 1986).

missionary effort. National assemblies include the names and nationalities of pioneers in their annual reports and the pioneers are considered to be a valuable resource. Most of the assemblies around the world would not have taken root had it not been for a coordinated international effort. Some national assemblies submit requests to have pioneers sent to them; other assemblies receive quantitative goals with respect to the number of pioneers they should commission. These goals are formulated in the "year plans" which were institutionalized by Shoghi Effendi.

The table opposite shows a statistical summary of the Seven Year Plan, 1979-1986, when a total of 3,694 international pioneers were commissioned. As is evident from the table's second row listing the number of pioneers laboring on a given continent, Europe received the lion's share out of all the continents.

However, if evaluated against cold, quantitative facts, Europe appears to have produced a meager return for the investment, as shown by the table's second set of data—the increase in membership per continent. Europe's growth was the lowest. However, the Europeans were active in sending out more of its own pioneers—the highest of all continents—if measured against the number of resident Baha'is per continent.

Pioneering has increased considerably in subsequent years. During the Three Year Plan, 1993-96, as many as 11,770 international pioneers were called, among whom 2,109 were from Europe.[22]

Missions at International Events

In line with the international outlook of Baha'i, a good share of its resources has been invested in international conferences and events, maintaining a particularly high profile at the NGO (Non-governmental Organization) events in connection with the eight United Nations world conferences from 1990 to 1996.[23] During the Social Summit in Copenhagen in 1995, Baha'is participated in the NGO exhibition at the former navel base of Copenhagen, about a mile from the official summit.[24] Inside the exhibition hall were two booths staffed by volunteers in distinctive blue sweatshirts emblazoned with "Bahá'í World Citizen" on the back. The Baha'is also arranged a number of special events and, for example, performed a ballet at the Global Village hall on 6 March with the theme "A Focus on World Citizenship and Global Prosperity."

The Baha'i participation at the 1995 Social Summit was only possible because of more than 250 volunteers who came to Copenhagen to assist.[25] In the years before and after the summit, people volunteered as full-time, unpaid administrative assistants with the secretariat of the Danish Baha'i community. The mission activities at the Social Summit were, in fact, rather demanding on the community's available resources.

Firesides

In day-to-day mission work, Baha'is have developed a particular method that is not as resource demanding and that has become an established and popular method of proselytizing the world over. The "fireside," as it is known, is held in private homes. From three to ten people, including non-member friends, converse over tea, coffee, and cookies. Someone may speak briefly on a prearranged topic, but the meeting is intended to be informal and open. It provides an opportunity for Baha'is to explain principles of the religion to proselytes and novices and to talk among themselves about a particular text or principle on a more advanced level. Although the presence of non-Baha'is is desirable, it is not crucial for the proceedings of the fireside.

A variant of the fireside is the "open house," often held at the local Baha'i center. As with firesides, a speaker introduces a topic as a prelude to a question and answer session. The format is, of course, less private than at a fireside. It is usually publicly advertised.

According to my studies, firesides play an important role in the recruitment of new Baha'is, at least in Denmark. About 40 percent of Danish Baha'is reported firesides to be an important element in their conversion. However, it takes many firesides to convert a single investigator, and if we extrapolate from a study of dropout rates among North American Baha'is, most visitors probably never convert. The study found that more than 80 percent of those who had participated in Baha'i meetings eventually stopped attending.[26] Data from Denmark suggest that less than 1 percent of the firesides led to successful recruitment. Were it not for their social and educational functions, firesides may not be viewed as a particularly fruitful strategy. However, firesides present a distinct advantage over a public mission. They are a low-cost method of carrying out mission activity, with the additional advantage of serving the social and educational needs within the group. Baha'is can therefore afford to arrange many of these.

SOCIAL DEVELOPMENT PROJECTS

In 1983 the Universal House of Justice initiated a policy of encouraging Baha'is to engage in social and economic development projects. Such grass-roots activities were meant to be a reinforcement of Baha'i missions.[27] The year the policy was announced, Baha'is were also encouraged to render service to "voluntary non-sectarian organizations."[28] The

Universal House of Justice expounded on this in 1985: "The time has come for the Bahá'í community to become more involved in the life of the society around it."[29]

Most of the social and economic development projects Baha'is engage in have been simple and temporary endeavors such as planting trees or sponsoring health camps. In 1997-98 Baha'is estimated that they were involved in some 1,460 projects of this kind.[30] But there were three hundred permanent projects as well, mostly in support of schools but also programs in health care, immunization, prevention of drug abuse, or protection of the environment.

In Banjul, Gambia, a Baha'i computer school is operated by an American pioneer. I visited the school in February 1999. The missionary, through his connections in the United States, obtained out-of-date but usable computers to offer a free three-month computer course for students with an A average in their local schools. It became an immediate success, with long waiting lists to the present. The school offers needed skills and improved qualifications for the students when they enter the job market. The classes were held at the Baha'i center where pamphlets on the Baha'i religion were available to interested students and, in some of the lessons, students were given Baha'i texts to work from. I was informed that during the last course, two students converted.

As with Christianity and Islam, education and conversion are the twin sisters of efficient missions. They offer potential converts not just the prospect of knowing the truth but also a chance to improve their lives.

WORKING THROUGH
INTERNATIONAL ORGANIZATIONS

More than five hundred NGOs have an advisory status with the United Nations Economic and Social Council

(ECOSOC).[31] Since 1970, the Baha'i International Community has enjoyed recognition from the ECOSOC, and this affiliation has given it a platform from which to seek influence in world development.[32]

Among the groups that participate with the United Nations, Baha'is are remarkable in their explicit belief that their religious teachings have a role in guiding international relations and politics. The religion has used the ECOSOC platform to address governments and the United Nations system in a series of statements on issues of global concern. The first and most significant statement in this regard was *The Promise of World Peace,* issued by the Universal House of Justice in 1985. It denounced the materialistic side of both capitalism and communism and promoted Baha'i principles of unity and equality.[33] Ten years later another statement, *Turning Point for All Nations,* was issued on the occasion of the fiftieth anniversary of the United Nations.[34] This document went more deeply into a review of current world affairs with specific recommendations for strengthening the U.N. system, promoting and protecting fundamental human rights, and advancing the status of women. According to Baha'is, these statements engage people—leaders and citizens alike—in becoming aware of the concept of world citizenship and in supporting an expanded international order. In a separate document, the Baha'is elaborated on world citizenship as an incarnation of a global ethic for sustainable development.[35]

These messages represent an attempt to extricate from Baha'i doctrine a detailed political program for global civilization. The religion thus aims beyond mere support of liberal democratic internationalism.[36] This is clearly seen from the concluding statement in the book, *Transition to a Global Society:*

The approach is to go beyond the democratic system of
election ... to a system incorporating several new principles
of which perhaps the two most important are a spiritual dimension, and a process of consultation rather than democratic debate. The spiritual dimension ... means that elected
government is responsible first to God rather than to the
electorate. In practice, this means a holistic viewpoint, em-
bracing not only the interests of the present but of the future, and of the environment as well as humanity. It means a
focus on creating conditions that maximize opportunity for
every man, woman, and child on the planet to develop his
or her full potential, physical, intellectual, and above all,
spiritual.[37]

The above viewpoint is not an anomalous sentiment. A
volume of the annual yearbook, *The Bahá'í World,* contained
two essays that criticized the idea of democracy based on
secular liberalism. The authors both asserted that universal
values need to be based on spirituality.[38]

With the idea that "elected government is responsible
first to God rather than to the electorate," Baha'is attack a
core aspect of the Enlightenment which for more than two
hundred years has been one of the cornerstones of democracies in the west. It is the principle of the separation of religious and political doctrines and institutions which means
that religion should not provide absolute guidelines for the
organization of society. In the future civilization foreseen by
Baha'is, secular law should therefore be subordinate to higher Baha'i principles. According to Shoghi Effendi, these are
not "an idle imitation of any form of absolutistic ecclesiasti-
cal government, whether it be the Papacy, the Imamate, or
any other similar institution." The difference, he maintained,
was that the right of legislation would be conferred to elected representatives.[39] However, the legislature would not

"be regarded as purely democratic in character inasmuch as the basic assumption which requires all democracies to depend fundamentally upon getting their mandate from the people is altogether lacking in this Dispensation."[40]

This view of the ultimate relationship between religion and government places Baha'is firmly in the Shi'ite tradition of merging religious and political administration. In the future Baha'i society, Baha'i institutions would, in principle, represent both spheres, as indicated above. This issue is debated among Baha'i intellectuals, and some claim that in his writings, Baha'u'llah did advocate what in western political tradition is called the separation of church and state.[41] But other authors, clearly representing the Baha'i establishment, have a different point of view, as shown above. Still, these differences involve interpretations of what Baha'u'llah intended for a distant-future state. As I have concluded elsewhere, Baha'is today are firmly attached to liberal political values, and only in doctrine does the Universal House of Justice support the idea that specific religious laws may in the future become a constitutional basis for society.[42] In its aspirations then, rather than in actual practice, Baha'i can resemble some of the fundamentalist currents within Judaism, Christianity, and Islam.

5.

Schism, Opposition, and Persecution

The Babi movement represented a radical trend among the Shi'ites. The Bab's break with Shi'i Islam in 1848 was a major schism, the wounds of which have never healed. Like other radical movements, Babism and Baha'i later went through several schisms which in turn gave birth to splinter groups in fierce opposition to mainstream Baha'i. Seen from a Muslim perspective, the Baha'is themselves are a splinter group based on a heretical doctrine, namely, the claim that there was a prophet after Muhammad.

SCHISMS SINCE THE BAB

In the period after the Bab's execution in 1850, the Babi movement began to disintegrate under Subh-i-Azal's leadership. Several other Babis stepped forward to claim competing spiritual authority, some declaring themselves to be the prophet promised by the Bab, "him whom God shall make manifest."[1] But none of these contenders was able to gain substantial acceptance and the majority continued to acknowledge the leadership of Subh-i-Azal.

A more serious schism occurred in 1866 when Baha'-u'llah claimed that he was "him whom God shall make manifest," implying that Subh-i-Azal should pay allegiance to him. The majority of the Babis accepted Baha'u'llah's claim, and the Azalis were reduced to a conservative minority group. Subh-i-Azal and his family were exiled to Cyprus, where he remained to his death in 1912. He made no attempt to organize a religious community in Famagusta, and the local population simply regarded him as a Muslim holy man.[2] The Azalis in Iran were soon outnumbered by Baha'is and their influence waned, although some of them played a role in the constitutional revolution of 1905. When Subh-i-Azal died, he was given a Turkish Muslim funeral, confirming that the Azali community in Cyprus no longer existed as an organized body.[3]

A small shrine adorns Subh-i-Azal's grave on the outskirts of Famagusta, Cyprus. I visited it in February 1996 and found that a grandson of Subh-i-Azal, then an old man of eighty-six years, was acting as the caretaker of the rather neglected shrine. A local Baha'i told me that in the 1960s, they received a visit from a wealthy Iranian woman who flew to the island and claimed to be a relative of the deceased. It was she who arranged for the shrine.

The next schism came when Abdu'l-Baha was challenged by his half-brother Muhammad-Ali, whose followers had considerable influence in the Akko area. The opposition was strengthened when the successful missionary to the United States, Ibrahim Kheiralla, broke from Abdu'l-Baha and most of the American Baha'is in 1900. Kheiralla organized his followers as "Behaists" and joined forces with Muhammad-Ali. The group does not exist anymore. In the Akko area, the followers of Muhammad-Ali have been reduced to six families who have no common organized religious activities.[4]

Shoghi Effendi's leadership was challenged by family members, and in the process of gaining control over the

Baha'i community, he excommuniced virtually all of Baha'-u'llah's descendants, as discussed in chapter 2.[5] Apparently none of the descendants tried to organize a competing group of Baha'is. A cousin of Shoghi Effendi, Ruhi Afnan, published two books after he was excommunicated, but the contents were compatible with established Baha'i concepts.[6] In the 1920s, the American Baha'i Ruth White opposed Shoghi Effendi and his Administrative Order. She became convinced that Abdu'l-Baha's will had been forged in a conspiracy between Muhammad-Ali and Shoghi Effendi, the former having been the one in effective control.[7] White won acceptance among some German Baha'is, and after World War II, her ideas continued in Germany through Hermann Zimmer, founder of the World Union for Universal Religion and Universal Peace.[8] His group has been a rallying point for "Free Baha'is" around the world ever since. Their number is uncertain but probably not more than a few hundred.

A more recent proponent of White's and Zimmer's refutation of the disputed will is Francesco Ficicchia who wrote a monograph in 1981 on the historical development of Baha'i and its institutions.[9] Written in German, the book seems to have gained some acceptance as a standard work in German-speaking countries. It spurred three Baha'i apologists to write a critical review of 685 pages which, if anything, demonstrated the sensitivity among Baha'is to the issue of opposition to the leadership.[10]

In the late 1920s, Ahmad Sohrab, Abdu'l-Baha's former secretary and interpreter, broke with the New York Baha'is when he and Julie Chanler formed the New History Society and, in 1939, opened their own Baha'i bookshop.[11] Shoghi Effendi brought suit against them to prevent them from using the word Baha'i. However, courts ruled that no group of believers can monopolize the name of a religion.[12]

Shoghi Effendi died in 1957, and the leadership of Baha'i was assumed by a self-appointed council of nine men called "the Custodians." One of them, Charles Mason Remey, declared in 1960 that he was the Guardian of Orthodox Baha'is. His group became known as "Baha'is under the Hereditary Guardianship." Even before Remey's death in 1974, his followers had begun to split into smaller groups, the largest of which was led by Joel B. Marangella (1918-) who claimed that Remey had appointed him to be the third guardian. On 25 August 1980, I interviewed Marangella's son, Joel Jani Marangella (1947-), and it was evident from the interview that Orthodox Baha'is was an organization that lacked any communal religious life. Another Remeyite group, "Baha'is under the Provisions of the Covenant," was founded by Leland Jensen (1913-1996) in Montana. Jensen prophesied that a nuclear attack would be launched on 29 April 1980 that would annihilate one-third of humankind. Before and after that date, three researchers conducted interviews with Jensen's followers in order to gauge their reactions to failed prophecy.[13]

In Indonesia in 1962 or 1963, Jamshid Maani of Iran declared himself to be the next manifestation of God after Baha'u'llah, calling himself "the Man," leader of "Faith in God."[14] An American Baha'i, John Carré, became the spokesperson for the Man and organized the American followers as the "House of Mankind." But in the 1970s Carré disassociated from the Man, and soon thereafter the movement ceased to exist.[15]

INTERNAL DISPUTES AND OPPOSITION

Since the mid-1970s the study of Babism and Baha'i has grown considerably. Most scholars in this field are Baha'is or former Baha'is. Their academic activities have now and then led to internal disputes concerning the issue of academic freedom. At the core of the disputes is the practice laid down by Shoghi Effendi that any Baha'i writing on a religious topic must submit his or her material for approval before it is published.[16] This not only applies to inspirational literature but also to academic works.

The background for the review policy was summarized in a letter from the Universal House of Justice to a group of young Baha'is who in 1978 were discussing ethics in scholarship:

> The principle of the harmony of science and religion means not only that religious teachings should be studied with the light of reason and evidence as well as of faith and inspiration, but also that everything in this creation, all aspects of human life and knowledge, should be studied in the light of revelation as well as that of purely rational investigation.[17]

In other words, the Universal House of Justice took a clear position in the conflict between academic freedom and acceptance of religious premises: the former must yield to the latter. In a reminder of the policy in 1993, the Universal House of Justice reiterated the same position.[18] It is hardly surprising that this policy has led to internal disputes and that these have occasionally surfaced in academic journals.[19] In principle, the core tension between doctrinal faith and academic freedom scholars may face from any religion, whether or not the leadership has adopted a prepublication review policy.

The Internet has provided another forum for scholarly discussion, which is not subject to prepublication review. However, Baha'i officials have monitored Baha'i discussion groups on the Internet and have reprimanded those who have aired complaints or circulated letters of petition.[20] As a result, some of the participants have resigned their membership. Others have decided to keep a low profile.

It is obvious that the leadership runs the risk of bad publicity with a policy that violates scholarly standards. However, the critics are very few and isolated and do not represent an organized or united front, so the sensitivity toward internal critique seems out of proportion to any potential threat. It might be partly explained as fear that another schism could emerge, fueled by a liberal critique. As history has thus far shown, Baha'is have succeeded in maintaining a monolithic organization through resolute excommunications and isolation of the opposition.

PERSECUTIONS

Since the time of the Babi fights of 1848-1853, Baha'is have suffered from a strained relationship with the Muslim majority in Iran. During some periods, overt persecution has been unleashed upon the Baha'is, while at other times the situation has been more relaxed and the Baha'is have been more-or-less tolerated, in particular during the regime of the last shah. Baha'is tend to be better educated than the average Iranian, and under the last shah, many of them were employed in education and health care or were even appointed to high government posts.

The Islamacist and Babi scholar Denis MacEoin predicts that the tension created by the Baha'i view of messianic Shi'ism will continue.[21] Baha'is envision a new world unified under one religion in line with Shi'ite eschatology. The difference is that Baha'is are ready to create that new world now because the redeemer, the Imam returned in the person of the Bab, has already made his appearance. It is a position that Shi'ites cannot accept because the return of the

Imam implies the end of Islam. MacEoin points out that in the eyes of the ulama, Baha'i also represents concepts of modernity such as equality of the sexes that run counter to the traditions the ulama attempted to restore in the 1979 revolution.[22]

The situation for Iranian Baha'is turned worse than ever in the wake of the revolution.[23] The constitution of the new Islamic Republic of Iran distinguished—as the earlier constitution did—between "religions of the book" and other religions. Besides Muslims, Zoroastrians, Jews, and Christians were considered members of legally recognized religions, while Baha'is—the largest religious minority with approximately 300,000 members in Iran—were excluded. This legal exclusion, mirroring the infamous Nürnberg laws of 1935 Germany, by relegating Baha'is to the second-class status of "unprotected infidels," with all the consequences that may imply, provided the basis for denying them civil rights. Most of the laws depriving Baha'is of civil and human rights were already in place before the revolution but were not in use. It is interesting but sad to see the lengths to which dictatorial governments will search for even the thinnest legal justification to harass an unwanted minority.

One efficient way to persecute a minority group is to deprive them of education and employment, and several steps were taken in this direction as summarized below:

- In 1979 a decree was issued barring Baha'i students and professors from studying or teaching at Iranian universities.
- In 1979 the government began a systematic dismissal of Baha'i civil servants.
- That same year the Ministry of Education dismissed all Baha'i teachers.

- Early in the 1980s the trading licenses of Baha'i businesses were revoked, the assets of Baha'i businesses confiscated, and bank accounts of most Baha'i businessmen frozen.
- Baha'i farmers were denied admission to the farmers' cooperatives.
- By 1982 practically all Baha'i public servants were out of work. In addition, their pensions had been rescinded.
- In 1984 former Baha'i civil servants were told to repay in full their salaries from the entire course of their careers.

Through arbitrary confiscation, looting, and destruction of property beginning in 1979, the Baha'i economy was ruined:

- In March 1979 the historic residence of the Bab in Shiraz was confiscated and given to a Muslim cleric. In September a group led by mullahs and officials of the Department of Religious Affairs destroyed the house. Since then, other Baha'i sites have been destroyed.
- Baha'i cemeteries were bulldozed and the graves dug up.
- Thousands of private Baha'i homes were confiscated.
- Baha'i community properties were transferred to the state.
- A major Baha'i savings company with 15,000 shareholders and investors was assumed by the government.

Bloody persecutions have occurred on a less wide scale but with more severe consequences. Since the revolution, almost 1,000 Baha'is have been placed in prison, with or without a trial, where they have been beaten, whipped, had their fingernails and teeth extracted, and have been forced to witness the torture of family members and friends. Many have reported pressure to recant their faith and convert to Islam. This would seem to demonstrate beyond doubt that they have been persecuted because of religious beliefs.

The charges range from apostasy and heresy to holding unauthorized meetings for youth, holding meetings in private houses, organizing children's art exhibits, Zionism, and the sexual crimes of prostitution, adultery, and immorality. The charges of Zionism and of being an imperialist agent and spy stem from the fact that the Baha'i World Centre is located within the borders of Israel. When Baha'is go on pilgrimage, it is to Israel, and when they send money, it is to the Baha'i World Centre in Israel. I was told by an Iranian woman that whenever a news report mentions the arrest of a Zionist spy, everyone in Iran knows that this means a member of the Baha'i religion. The accusation is made so often that "Baha'i" and "Zionist agent" have become synonymous.

The charges of immorality and adultery are founded in the fact that until recently Iran did not recognize Baha'i marriages. This meant that Baha'i children, by strict definition, were illegitimate. The lack of recognition implied that Baha'is who were imprisoned did not have the right to receive visits from spouses and that a husband or wife could not claim the body of a deceased spouse. Baha'i marriages are still not recognized, but the Iranian courts have since allowed couples to register their marriage without identifying their religious affiliation. This is an important first step toward a possibly more relaxed ambiance for the Baha'is.

Since 1979 more than two hundred Baha'is have been executed or killed in prison. Most often the sentencing has resulted from a summary mock trial, if a prisoner is tried at

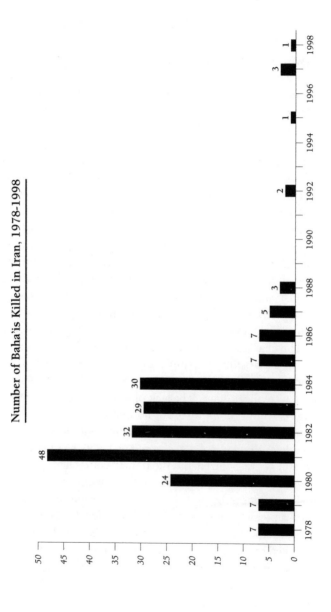

Number of Baha'is Killed in Iran, 1978-1998

all. Fifteen additional Baha'is have disappeared and are presumed to be dead. It is a noteworthy token of the destructive strategy of the Iranian regime that half of the executed Baha'is were members of local and national spiritual assemblies. However, any kind of Baha'i activity can be reason for execution. In June 1983 ten Baha'i women, including two teenage girls, were hanged for holding children's classes for Baha'i youth.

As can be seen from the chart on page 72, the executions reached a peak in the early 1980s. Most observers feel that appeals from international organizations and the news media had a dampening effect on the regime. All eighteen resolutions of the U.N. Commission on Human Rights regarding Iran have condemned the deprivations against Baha'is. Since 1985 the U.N. General Assembly has approved thirteen resolutions denouncing Iran for human rights violations, but the killings have not entirely stopped, as seen from the chart.

NAJIS AND RUMORS OF IMMORALITY

The stated reasons for actions against the Baha'is are many and varied. However, persecution would not be orchestrated by the government if there were not popular sympathy for it. I interviewed a number of Iranian Baha'is in the autumn of 1982 to learn more about how they are perceived by the greater population. The following are examples.

Central to Shi'i Islam is a concept known as "najis," which means religiously unclean.[24] Most Iranians know little more about Baha'is than that the Baha'i prophet came after Muhammad, which makes the adherents heretics and najis. There are other minorities who are najis: Jews, for example. Animals can be najis: pigs are, of course, while a cow is not. As is known from other cultures, that which is unclean is contagious and it is therefore important to avoid contact with whatever is infected. For instance, it might be dangerous to accept tea in a Baha'i home. In fact, some Iranians believe that when Baha'is serve tea, it is the means to make unsuspecting victims accept their faith.

An Iranian refugee told me about a mullah who confiscated the apartment of a wealthy Baha'i family. Before the mullah entered the dwelling, even before he had the furniture and carpets removed, he took a garden hose and sprayed down the inside to make sure that everything was clean. In his mind, the apartment and everything in it were najis. A young girl told a similar story. During the war with Iraq, students in her school were encouraged to donate blood. Her teacher informed her that she was an exception and that her unclean blood was of no use to the soldiers.

It should be stressed that many Muslim Iranians ridicule the concept of najis, saying it is believed only by peasants. However, the incidents cited above demonstrate how widespread the belief is, even within a middle-class setting. Najis explains why Baha'is have been excluded from medical and teaching professions in particular.

Some Muslim Iranians believe that Baha'is live immoral lives, perhaps because of the Baha'i principle that men and women must have the same possiblities and rights. Unlike the tradition of the mosque where men and women are segregated, Baha'i men and women sit together at religious gatherings. Baha'i women tended not to wear the chador before the revolution, and this was seen by orthodox clergy and many common citizens as an affront to morality.

This has indeed given rise to many fanciful rumors in Iran. One is that Baha'i fathers and daughters indulge in sexual relationships, as do mothers and sons, according to this rumor. I have heard that the gossip among some Shi'ites

is that Baha'i religious gatherings involve group sex, that—
even more astonishing—the lights are turned off and men
put on the women's clothes and women put on the men's
clothes!

For the sake of good order, let me emphasize that there is
no evidence to support any such rumors. They seem to arise
from the already ambiguous feelings which some Muslim
Iranians have toward Baha'is. Together with the concept of
najis, the knowledge that these and other rumors circulate
may help us to understand why so many Iranians seem to
accept the persecution of this law-abiding religious minority.

Notes

CHAPTER 1. THE BAHAI'S

1. In accordance with a recent trend among scholars of Baha'i, the author has chosen not to use diacritical marks in words transcribed from Persian or Arabic except in book titles and quotations.

CHAPTER 2. THE EMERGENCE AND HISTORICAL
DEVELOPMENT OF THE BAHA'I RELIGION

1. The following section is based in part on Abbas Amanat, *Resurrection and Renewal: The Making of the Babi Movement in Iran, 1844-1850* (Ithaca and London: Cornell University Press, 1989), and Moojan Momen, *An Introduction to Shi'i Islam: The History and Doctrines of Twelver Shi'ism* (New Haven: Yale University Press, 1985). A short, well-written overview of contemporary Shi'ism is found in Denis MacEoin, "The Shi'i Establishment in Modern Iran," *Islam in the Modern World,* eds. MacEoin and Ahmed Al-Shahi (London: Croom Helm, 1983), 88-108.

2. Amanat, *Resurrection and Renewal,* 89-102; Denis MacEoin, "Early Shaykhí Reactions to the Báb and His Claims," *Studies in Bábí and Bahá'í History,* vol. 1, ed. Moojan Momen (Los Angeles: Kalimat Press, 1982), 1-47. Dates followed by "AH" are according to the Muslim calendar. Year one is 622 CE, the year Muhammad fled from Mecca to Medina ("AH" means "Anno Hijrae"—the year of the migration). Note that because the Muslim year is lunar, which is eleven days shorter than the solar year, translation from AH to CE ("Common Era") is complicated.

3. Peter Smith, "A Note on Babi and Baha'i Numbers in Iran," *Iranian Studies* 17/2-3 (1984): 295-301.

4. Edward Granville Browne, "The Bábís of Persia: Their Literature and Doctrines," *Journal of the Royal Asiatic Society* 21 (1889): 881-1,009.

5. The central Baha'i law book is Baha'u'lláh's *Kitáb-i-Aqdas: The Most Holy Book* (Haifa: Baha'i World Centre, 1992). Some of the Bab's laws and ordinances were abrogated in this work, including the rules of prohibition and uncleanliness. A list is given on p. 159 in the *Kitáb-i-Aqdas*.

6. D. M. MacEoin, "Bab, Sayyed 'Alí Moḥammad Šīrāzī," *Encyclopædia Iranica*, vol. 3, ed. Ehsan Yarshater (London: Routledge & Kegan Paul, 1988), 278-84.

7. Browne, "The Bábís of Persia."

8. Denis MacEoin, "A Note on the Numbers of Babi and Baha'i Martyrs in Iran," *Bahá'í Studies Bulletin* 2 (Sept. 1983): 84-8.

9. Peter Smith, "Millenarianism in the Babi and Baha'i Religions," *Millennialism and Charisma*, ed. Roy Wallis (Belfast: Queen's University, 1982), 231-83; Peter Smith, *The Babi and Baha'i Religions: From Messianic Shi'ism to a World Religion* (Cambridge: Cambridge University Press and George Ronald, 1987), 43.

10. Edward G. Browne, ed. and trans., *The Tárikh-i-Jadíd or New History of Mírzá 'Alí Muḥammad the Báb, by Mírzá Ḥuseyn of Hamadán* (Cambridge: Cambridge University Press, 1893), 55.

11. The sources regarding the date are conflicting. See Amanat, *Resurrection and Renewal,* 402; John Walbridge, *Sacred Acts, Sacred Space, Sacred Time* (Oxford: George Ronald, 1996), 229-30.

12. Several eyewitnesses described these tortures, the most famous being the 29 August 1852 account by an Austrian officer, published in a military magazine. It was translated by Edward G. Browne in *Materials for the Study of the Bábí Religion* (Cambridge: Cambridge University Press, 1918), 267-71, and reproduced with fuller biographical details in Moojan Momen, *The Bábí and Bahá'í Religions, 1844-1944: Some Contemporary Western Accounts* (Oxford: George Ronald, 1981), 132-4.

13. The word dervish is derived from the Persian for Sufi, a Muslim mystic.

14. Shoghi Effendi, *God Passes By* (Wilmette, Illinois: Baha'i Publishing Trust, 1995), 151-5.

15. Walbridge, *Sacred Acts,* 238. The quotation is from Shoghi Effendi, *God Passes By,* 151.

16. Adib Taherzadeh, *The Revelation of Bahá'u'lláh: Adrianople 1863-68* (Oxford: George Ronald, 1977), 301-5; Smith, *Babi and Baha'i Religions,* 67.

17. The word Baha'i is also used as an adjective, e.g., "Baha'i Prayers." In this book I also use the noun Baha'i as the short term for the Baha'i religion. The Baha'is themselves use the term Bahá'í Faith and retain the diacritical marks in transcribing from the Persian or Arabic.

18. Walbridge, *Sacred Acts,* 47, 116.

19. *Kitáb-i-Aqdas*, 1992. A previous translation into English by two Protestant missionaries is not considered authoritative. See William McElwee Miller and Earl E. Elder, eds., trans., *Al-Kitáb al-Aqdas: Or the Most Holy Book by Mírzá Husayn 'Alí Bahá'u'lláh* (London: Royal Asiatic Society, 1961).

20. *A Synopsis and Codification of the Kitáb-i-Aqdas, the Most Holy Book of Bahá'u'lláh* (Haifa: Baha'i World Centre, 1973); Shoghi Effendi, ed., *Gleanings from the Writings of Bahá'u'lláh* (Wilmette: Baha'i Publishing Trust, 1983), an authoritative compilation of Baha'u'llah's writings; it was issued for the first time in 1935 and is a standard scriptural volume for all Baha'is.

21. Juan R. I. Cole, *Modernity and the Millennium: The Genesis of the Baha'i Faith in the Nineteenth-Century Middle East* (New York: Columbia University Press, 1998).

22. Abdu'l-Baha, *The Secret of Divine Civilization* (Wilmette: Baha'i Publishing Trust, 1990). The Persian text was lithographed in Bombay in 1882.

23. Smith, *Babi and Baha'i Religions,* 124-8. From information gathered during my fieldwork at the Baha'i World Centre in 1987 and 1988-89, my impression is that there are still disputes with descendants of Muhammad-Ali over family relics.

24. The Baha'i World Centre is described in greater detail in chapter 4.

25. The doctrine of the covenant, its historical development, and its implications are extensively discussed in Adib Taherzadeh, *The Covenant of Bahá'u'lláh* (Oxford: George Ronald, 1992). The Day of the Covenant is celebrated on 26 November. See also Walbridge, *Sacred Acts,* 244-5.

26. David Piff and Margit Warburg, "Enemies of the Faith: Rumours and Anecdotes as Self-Definition in the Baha'i Religion," *New Religions and New Religiosity,* eds. Eileen Barker and Margit Warburg (Aarhus: Aarhus University Press, 1998), 66-82.

27. Many of Abdu'l-Baha's letters and talks have been collected and published by the Baha'i World Centre.

28. Abdu'l-Baha's public addresses during this tour were later (1922-25) compiled and issued by the American Baha'is. See *The Promulgation of Universal Peace: Talks Delivered by 'Abdu'l-Bahá during His Visit to the United States and Canada in 1912* (Wilmette: Baha'i Publishing Trust, 1998).

29. Robert H. Stockman, "The Bahá'í Faith in England and Germany, 1900-1913," *World Order* 27 (Spring 1996): 31-42.

30. Smith, *Babi and Baha'i Religions,* 117-126.

31. These conflicts are discussed in greater detail in chapter 5.

32. Shoghi Effendi, *God Passes By,* 326.

33. *Principles of Bahá'í Administration: A Compilation* (London: Baha'i Publishing Trust, 1976). A detailed and up-to-date description of the procedures and by-laws of the various administrative bodies of the Administrative Order is found in *The Bahá'í World: An International Record, 1979-1983* (Haifa: Baha'i World Centre, 1986), 453-603.

34. Elections are held on the first day of Ridvan (21 April), and voters cast nine votes by secret ballot. Canvassing for particular candidates is not allowed. See *Principles of Bahá'í Administration,* 46-7.

35. See, e.g., Shoghi Effendi, *The World Order of Bahá'u'lláh: Selected Letters* (Wilmette: Baha'i Publishing Trust, 1991).

36. See introduction to *The Kitáb-i-Aqdas,* 9.

37. Walbridge, *Sacred Acts,* 21.

38. The most important messages from the Universal House of Justice are compiled and issued regularly by the Baha'i World Centre. These messages are considered authoritative and binding.

39. Even today, this issue gives rise to speculation and folklore among the Baha'is. See David Michael Piff, *Bahá'í Lore* (Oxford: George Ronald, 2000), 101-03.

40. Smith, *Babi and Baha'i Religions,* 130-1. The Remeyite and other splinter groups are described in greater detail in chapter 5.

CHAPTER 3. BAHA'I BELIEFS AND RITUALS

1. See, e.g., *The Bahá'í World: An International Record, 1993-94* (Haifa: Baha'i World Centre, 1994), 8.

2. Shoghi Effendi, *The World Order of Bahá'u'lláh: Selected Letters* (Wilmette: Baha'i Publishing Trust, 1991), 204.

3. This will be further expounded in chapter 4.

4. *Tablets of Bahá'u'lláh Revealed after the Kitáb-i-Aqdas* (Wilmette: Baha'i Publishing Trust, 1995), 127.

5. John Walbridge, *Sacred Acts, Sacred Space, Sacred Time* (Oxford: George Ronald, 1996), 185.

6. *The Kitáb-i-Aqdas: The Most Holy Book* (Haifa: Baha'i World Centre, 1992), 25.

7. Ibid., 207-8.

8. *Principles of Baha'i Administration: A Compilation* (London: Baha'i Publishing Trust, 1976), 52.

9. Walbridge, *Sacred Acts,* 209-10.

10. Walbridge, ibid., 211. In the annual statistical reports to the Baha'i World Centre, observance of Nineteen Day Feasts is reported.

11. *Kitáb-i-Aqdas,* 19-21.

12. *Principles of Bahá'í Administration,* 8-9.

13. Walbridge, *Sacred Acts,* 30-55.

14. As Walbridge notes, when Baha'u'llah and Abdu'l-Baha changed the qiblih from Mecca to Bahji, it was a strong signal of independence from Islam. See *Sacred Acts,* 47.

15. The only prescribed prayer to be said aloud in congregation is the invocation for the dead, which is part of the Baha'i funeral ceremony discussed later in this chapter.

16. Walbridge, *Sacred Acts,* 46.

17. *Kitáb-i-Aqdas,* 145-8.

18. *Kitáb-i-Aqdas,* 179; Walbridge, *Sacred Acts,* 67-71.

19. *Kitáb-i-Aqdas,* 179.

20. *Principles of Bahá'í Administration,* 9.

21. William S. Hatcher and J. Douglas Martin, *The Bahá'í Faith: The Emerging Global Religion* (San Francisco: Harper and Row, 1989), 158-159; Walbridge, *Sacred Acts,* 45-55, 81-2.

22. *Kitáb-i-Aqdas,* 43.

23. Walbridge, *Sacred Acts,* 77-8.

24. I visited the cemetery 23 March 1993 and 23 August 1998 and interviewed the caretaker. In the first half of 1998, he had registered more than 6,000 visitors.

25. Much of the information on the pilgrimage is based on my fieldwork at the Baha'i World Centre in 1987 and 1988-89.

26. Wendi Momen, ed., *A Basic Bahá'í Dictionary* (Oxford: George Ronald, 1991), 198.

27. Walbridge, *Sacred Acts,* 134-5.

28. Margit Warburg, "Economic Rituals: The Structure and Meaning of Donations in the Baha'i Religion," *Social Compass* 40 (1993): 25-31. The following two pages are essentially based on this article.

29. *Principles of Bahá'í Administration,* 94.

CHAPTER 4. BAHAI'S IN THE WORLD

1. Eileen Barker, *The Making of a Moonie: Choice or Brainwashing?* (Oxford: Basil Blackwell, 1984), 27.

2. Membership data for England come from the Baha'i World Centre, June 1978. By comparison, an established religious group such as the Jehovah's Witnesses reported 126,297 members in 2000. See Andrew Holden, *Jehovah's Witnesses: Portrait of a Contemporary Religious Movement* (London: Routledge, 2002), 21. This number corresponds to less than 0.3 percent of the adult British population.

3. *The Bahá'í World: An International Record, 1996-97* (Haifa: Baha'i World Centre, 1998), 313, back cover.

4. During the British Baha'i Six Year Plan from 1944 to 1950, British pioneers constantly moved to secure groups of nine. See Phillip R. Smith, "The Development and Influence of the Bahá'í Administrative Order in Great Britain, 1914-1950," *Community*

Histories: Studies in the Bábí and Bahá'í Religions, vol. 6, ed. Richard Hollinger (Los Angeles: Kalimat Press, 1992), 206.

5. In Denmark, all Baha'is with unconfirmed addresses are put on a special list and are not reported as members.

6. In the U.S. there were 77,396 registered Baha'is in 1978, but only 62 percent of them had confirmed addresses. See Juan R. I. Cole, "The Baha'i Faith in America as Panopticon, 1963-1997," *Journal for the Scientific Study of Religion* 37 (1998): 234-48.

7. Shoghi Effendi, "The Spiritual Significance of the Mashriqu'l-Adhkár," *The Bahá'í World: An International Record, 1979-1983* (Haifa: Bahá'í World Centre, 1986), 569-70.

8. Horace Holley, foreword, "The Institution of the Mashriqu'l-Adhkár, ibid., 568.

9. "The Bahá'í Home (1958-2001)," http://www. kingdomproject. org/whats_kp/m_adhkar/bhome.html, accessed 8 Apr. 2003.

10. M. Momen, "The Baha'i Community of Ashkhabad: Its Social Basis and Importance in Baha'i History," *Cultural Change and Continuity in Central Asia,* ed. Shirin Akiner (London: Kegan Paul, 1991), 278-303.

11. V. Rafati, "The Bahai community of Ashkhabad (Ešgābād), *Encyclopedia Iranica,* vol. 3, ed. Ehsan Yarshater (London: Routledge & Kegan Paul, 1989), 460-1.

12. Baha'i chanting is melodious and recites sacred texts in Persian or Arabic, adapted from Islamic practices; R. Jackson Armstrong-Ingram, *Music, Devotions, and Mashriqu'l-Adhkár: Studies in Bábí and Bahá'í History,* vol. 4 (Los Angeles: Kalimat Press, 1987).

13. Shoghi Effendi, *God Passes By* (Wilmette: Baha'i Publishing Trust, 1995), 194.

14. "Lawḥ-i-Karmil," *Tablets of Bahá'u'lláh Revealed after the Kitáb-i-Aqdas* (Wilmette: Baha'i Publishing Trust, 1995), 3-5. Baha'u'llah's letters are referred to as tablets but were composed with ink and paper.

15. David S. Ruhe, *Door of Hope: A Century of the Bahá'í Faith in the Holy Land* (Oxford: George Ronald, 1986), 145.

16. Ibid., 154.

17. Adib Taherzadeh, *The Covenant of Bahá'u'lláh* (Oxford: George Ronald, 1992), 225-6.

18. Shoghi Effendi, *God Passes By,* 347.

19. There is a smaller copy of Baha'u'llah's portrait at the temple in Kampala, Uganda, among other sites, but is rarely shown to Baha'is and only after permission is granted from the Universal House of Justice (Interview with a local temple official in Kampala, 13 February 2000).

20. [Universal House of Justice], *The Seven Year Plan, 1979-1986: Statistical Report* (Haifa: [Baha'i World Centre], 1986), 1.

21. Margit Warburg, "Economic Rituals: The Structure and Meaning of Donations in the Baha'i Religion," *Social Compass* 40 (1993): 25-31. In his study of Baha'is in Atlanta, Georgia, Mike McMullen reported that in 1993, well over half (58 percent) of the members contributed to the so-called Arc Fund earmarked for projects on Mount Carmel. See Michael McMullen, *The Bahá'í: The Religious Construction of a Global Identity* (New Brunswick: Rutgers University Press, 2000), 83. However, a direct comparison between his and my figures is not possible.

22. [Universal House of Justice], *The Three Year Plan, 1993-1996: Summary of Achievements* ([Haifa], Baha'i World Centre, 1997).

23. The eight U.N. world conferences were the World Summit for Children, New York, 1990; United Nations Conference on Environment and Development, Rio de Janeiro, 1992; World Conference on Human Rights, Vienna, 1993; International Conference on Population and Development, Cairo, 1994; World Summit for Social Development, Copenhagen, 1995; Fourth World Conference on Women, Beijing, 1995; Second United Nations Conference on Human Settlements (Habitat II), Istanbul, 1996; and the World Food Summit, Rome, 1996.

24. The following is based on personal observations and material gathered during my visit to the NGO Forum '95 on 5 March of that year.

25. Press Release, Baha'i International Community, 6 March 1997.

26. Frederick Bird and William Reimer, "Participation Rates in New Religious and Parareligious Movements," *Of Gods and Men: New Religious Movements in the West,* ed. Eileen Barker (Macon: Mercer University Press, 1983), 215-38.

27. *Messages from the Universal House of Justice, 1963-1986: The Third Epoch of the Formative Age* (Wilmette: Baha'i Publishing Trust, 1996), 601-4.

28. Ibid., 611-12.

29. Universal House of Justice, *A Wider Horizon: Selected Messages of the Universal House of Justice, 1983-1992* (Riviera Beach, Florida: Palabra Publications, 1992), 148.

30. *The Bahá'í World: An International Record, 1997-98* (Haifa: Baha'i World Centre, 1999), 281-2.

31. United Nations, *Directory of Non-Governmental Organizations Associated with the Department of Public Information* (New York City: United Nations Department of Public Information, 1995). Examples of other religious NGOs are the Baptist World Alliance, Brahma Kumaris World Spiritual University, several Catholic organizations, the Conference of European Churches, the Greek Orthodox Archdiocese, Lutheran World Federation, Muslim World League, the Salvation Army, Soka Gakkai International, United Nations of Yoga, the World Jewish Congress, and the World Muslim Congress.

32. See survey articles in *The Bahá'í World: An International Record, 1979-1983* (Haifa: Baha'i World Centre, 1986).

33. Universal House of Justice, *The Promise of World Peace to the Peoples of the World* (Wilmette: Baha'i Publishing Trust, 1985). This was published as a beautiful booklet printed on thick buff paper with blue and gold ink.

34. *Turning Point for All Nations: A Statement of the Bahá'í International Community on the Occasion of the Fiftieth Anniversary of the United Nations* (New York: Baha'i International Community, 1995).

35. *World Citizenship: A Global Ethic for Sustainable Development* (New York: Baha'i International Community, 1998).

36. The following discussion is based on Margit Warburg, "Baha'i: A Religious Approach to Globalization," *Social Compass* 46 (1999): 47-56.

37. John Huddleston, "Perspectives, Purposes, and Brotherhood: A Spiritual Framework for a Global Society," *Transition to a Global Society,* eds. Suheil Bushrui, Iraj Ayman, and Ervin Laszlo (Oxford: Oneworld, 1993), 142-50.

38. Wendy M. Heller, "Covenant and the Foundations of Civil Society," and Ann Boyles, "World Watch," *The Bahá'í World: An International Record, 1995-96* (Haifa: Baha'i World Centre, 1997), 185-222; 223-40.

39. Shoghi Effendi, *The World Order of Bahá'u'lláh: Selected Letters* (Wilmette: Baha'i Publishing Trust, 1991), 153.

40. Ibid., 153.

41. See, e.g., Juan R. I. Cole, "Iranian Millenarianism and Democratic Thought in the Nineteenth Century," *International Journal of Middle East Studies* 24 (1992): 1-26; Sen McGlinn, "A Theology of the State from the Bahá'í Teachings," *Journal of Church and State* 41 (1999), 697-724.

42. Warburg, "Baha'i: A Religious Approach to Globalization."

CHAPTER 5. SCHISM, OPPOSITION, AND PERSECUTION

1. The Babi/Baha'i term for this prophet is the *man yuzhiruhu'lláh.* The Baha'is believe that Baha'u'llah was the *man yuzhiruhu'lláh.*

2. Moojan Momen, "The Cyprus Exiles," *Bahá'í Studies Bulletin* 5-6 (June 1991): 84-113.

3. Ibid., 97.

4. Erik Cohen, "The Bahá'í Community of Acre," *Folklore Research Center Studies* 3 (1972): 119-41.

5. Peter Smith, *The Babi and Baha'i Religions: From Messianic Shi'ism to a World Religion* (Cambridge: Cambridge University Press and George Ronald, 1987), 125.

6. William P. Collins, *Bibliography of English-Language Works on the Bábí and Bahá'í Faiths, 1844-1985* (Oxford: George Ronald, 1990), 295.

7. Smith, *Babi and Baha'i Religions,* 124.

8. J. Gordon Melton, "World Union of Universal Religion and Universal Peace," *Encyclopedia of American Religions,* 6th ed. (Detroit: Gale, 1999), 885.

9. Francesco Ficicchia, *Der Baha'ismus: Weltreligion der Zukunft? Geschichte, Lehre, und Organisation in kritischer Anfrage* (Stuttgart: Quell Verlag, 1981).

10. Udo Schaefer, Nicola Towfigh, and Ulrich Gollmer, *Des-*

information als Methode: Die Bahá'ismus Monographie des F. Fi-cicchia, Religionswissenschaftliche Texte und Studien, Band 6 (Hildesheim: Georg Olms Verlag, 1995), translated into English as *Making the Crooked Straight: A Contribution to Bahá'í Apologetics* (Oxford: George Ronald, 2000).

11. Smith, *Babi and Baha'i Religions,* 125.

12. Melton, "World Union," 885.

13. Robert Balch, Gwen Farnsworth, and Sue Wilkins, "When the Bombs Drop: Reactions to Disconfirmed Prophecy in a Millennial Sect," *Sociological Perspectives* 26 (1983), 137-58.

14. David Piff, personal communication, 2000.

15. Melton, "Faith of God," op. cit., 883.

16. "The Policy of Prepublication Review: On Behalf of the Universal House of Justice, Enclosed with a Letter to an Individual Dated 5 October 1993," *Bahá'í Studies Review* 3/2 (1993): 43-5.

17. Research Department, Bahá'í World Centre, "Ethics and Methodology," *Bahá'í Studies Review* 3/2 (1993): 39-42. These comments were enclosed in a letter of 3 January 1979 "to the participants in the Bahá'í Studies Seminar held in Cambridge on 30 September and 1 October 1978."

18. "The Policy of Prepublication Review," op. cit., 43-45; "Further Comments on Bahá'í Scholarship": From a Letter on Behalf of the Universal House of Justice Dated 19 October 1993," *Bahá'í Studies Review* 3/2 (1993): 46-9.

19. Two of the most detailed and important discussions of the detrimental effect of the review policy are: Denis MacEoin, "The Crisis in Babi and Baha'i Studies: Part of a Wider Crisis in Academic Freedom?" *British Society for Middle Eastern Studies Bulletin* 17 (1990): 55-61; Juan R. I. Cole, "The Baha'i Faith in America as Panopticon, 1963-1997," *Journal for the Scientific Study of Religion* 37 (1998): 234-48.

20. Universal House of Justice to all National Spiritual Assemblies, "Issues Related to the Study of the Baha'i Faith," 7 April 1999.

21. Denis MacEoin, "A People Apart: The Baha'i Community of Iran in the Twentieth Century," paper 4, Centre of Near and

Middle Eastern Studies, School of Oriental and African Studies, University of London, 1989, 27.

22. Denis MacEoin, "The Baha'is of Iran: The Roots of Controversy," *British Society for Middle Eastern Studies Bulletin* 14 (1988): 75-83.

23. A fact-oriented report on Iranian Baha'is after 1979 has been issued by the London-based Minority Rights Group. See Roger Cooper, *The Baha'is of Iran,* report no. 51 (London: Minority Rights Group, 1982). More recent facts are found in *The Bahá'í Question: Iran's Secret Blueprint for the Destruction of a Religious Community; an Examination of the Persecution of the Bahá'ís of Iran* (New York: Baha'i International Community, 1999). The following description of persecutions is based on these reports and material from Margit Warburg, *Iranske Dokumenter: Forfølgelsen af Bahá'ierne i Iran* (Copenhagen: Rhodos, 1985).

24. Eliz Sanasarian, *Religious Minorities in Iran* (Cambridge: Cambridge University Press, 2000), 23-4.

Bibliographical Note

Scholarship on Babism and Baha'i began in the 1860s and reached a peak at the turn of the twentieth century. The most outstanding figure of that period was the British orientalist Edward Granville Browne (1862-1926). From around 1920, academic studies declined to the point that only a few more works appeared until the late 1970s when a more permanent tradition developed.

Several books consider the Mid-Eastern context of Baha'i origins. Early Babism is treated in detail in Abbas Amanat, *Resurrection and Renewal: The Making of the Babi Movement in Iran, 1844-1850* (Ithaca and London: Cornell University Press, 1989). A comprehensive survey of the sources and a basic reference for any serious scholarship on Babism is Denis MacEoin, *The Sources for Early Bábí Doctrine and History* (Leiden, Netherlands: E. J. Brill, 1992). MacEoin has also published many articles on Shaykhism, Babism, and early Baha'i. A useful compilation of western sources is Moojan Momen, *The Bábí and Bahá'í Religions, 1844-1944* (Oxford: George Ronald, 1981). Juan R. I. Cole's *Modernity and the Millennium: The Genesis of the Baha'i Faith in the Nineteenth-Century Middle East* (New York: Columbia University Press, 1998) is an illuminating treatment of Baha'u'llah's writings in the context of the intellectual and political reform history of Iran and the Ottoman Empire in the nineteenth century.

Scholarship on Baha'i in modern western societies is more fragmented and seems to have proceeded along several not quite related tacks. Some of the works are community histories or surveys in the form of graduate theses. The most prominent books are Robert H. Stockman, *The Bahá'í Faith in America*, 2 vols.

(Wilmette: Bahá'í Publishing Trust, 1985; Oxford: George Ronald, 1995); Richard Hollinger, ed., *Community Histories*, vol. 6, Studies in the Bábí and Bahá'í Religions (Los Angeles: Kalimát Press, 1992); and Will C. van den Hoonaard, *The Origins of the Bahá'í Community of Canada, 1898-1948* (Waterloo: Wilfrid Laurier University Press, 1996).

No general history based on primary sources has yet been published, but sociologist Peter Smith has written *The Babi and Baha'i Religions: From Messianic Shi'ism to a World Religion* (Cambridge: Cambridge University Press and George Ronald, 1987). It analyzes the history of the Baha'i religion and the emergence of important motifs and is recognized as the standard work on Babi and Baha'i history to modern times. My own studies of Baha'i deal with contemporary demography, economy, and religious responses to globalization, which will be more extensively discussed in my forthcoming book, *Citizens of the World: A History and Sociology of the Baha'is from a Globalized Perspective*. John Walbridge's *Sacred Acts, Sacred Space, Sacred Time* (Oxford: George Ronald, 1996) is a thorough analysis of Baha'i beliefs, rituals, and the interpretation of Baha'i law as seen from historical and sociological perspectives.

Two official Baha'i histories have received quasi-doctrinal status. One was authored by a close associate of Baha'u'llah and was edited and translated into English by Shoghi Effendi as *The Dawn-Breakers* (Wilmette: Bahá'í Publishing Trust, 1932). Shoghi Effendi also wrote his own interpretation of the Babi and Baha'i history from 1844 to 1944 in *God Passes By* (Wilmette: Bahá'í Publishing Trust, 1944). William S. Hatcher's and J. Douglas Martin's *The Bahá'í Faith: The Emerging Global Religion* (San Francisco: Harper and Row, 1989) is a more recent survey of the history, beliefs, and practices of the religion from an inside perspective and in line with official views.

There are three useful handbooks: William P. Collins's *Bibliography of English-Language Works on the Bábí and Bahá'í Faiths, 1844-1985* (Oxford: George Ronald, 1990); Glenn Cameron's and Wendi Momen's *A Basic Bahá'í Chronology* (Oxford: George Ronald, 1996); and Peter Smith's *A Concise Encyclopedia of the Bahá'í Faith* (Oxford: Oneworld, 2000).

A comprehensive presentation of Baha'u'llah's writings and their theological meaning and implications is Adib Taherzadeh's four-volume *The Revelation of Bahá'u'lláh* (Oxford: George Ronald, 1975-1988). Many of the sacred writings from Baha'u'llah and other leading figures of the Baha'i religion have been translated and published in English.